BERTIE AND ME AND MILES TOO

Bertie and Me and Miles Too

Growing Up on a Nebraska Sandhill Ranch in the Early 1900s

Billie Lee Snyder Thornburg

THE OLD HUNDRED AND ONE PRESS

North Platte, Nebraska

Published by the Old 101 Press
13680 N Sandhill Drive
North Platte, NE 69101

Printed in the United State of America

Cover Design by Billy Pigati
Book Design by Kai Crozer
Edited by Ann Milton

Library of Congress Control Number: 2003108909
Thornburg, Billie Lee Snyder
Bertie and Me and Miles Too / by Billie Lee Snyder Thornburg
p. cm
Summary: Tells about kids growing up on a ranch in the Sandhills of Nebraska
from 1912 to 1927.
ISBN 0-9721613-3-3

To my beloved brother, Miles Snyder
1906 - 1997

*Miles in his late twenties. He's dressed to
court his future wife, Hollis Blackstone,
the schoolteacher at the school behind him.*

CONTENTS

A Note From the Author

I was talked into writing my first book, *Bertie and Me*. In fact, I was pushed into it. The further I got into the book, the more I thought people would not want to read that stuff. The only thing I felt that I was accomplishing was making Bertie feel good since I was admitting for the first that I was ornery to her when we were kids.

I was surprised and very pleased when readers told me they enjoyed reading the stories, some even identified with them. I realized I had a head full of history and so I wrote this second book.

I wish to thank Josee Forell, Valerie Paxton and Pattie Green Paxton for their help editing this book. They're wonderful relatives.

Thanks also to Vernon Combs for his great photos and information about the early roundups put on by the Combs Brothers (Vernon's father Arch and his Uncle Guy), and thanks to Jim Beckius for Model T photos from his incredible historical collection of early pictures.

Finally, I take this opportunity to tell my sister Bertie how much I love her and how much I appreciate her letting me write about her.

The Bert Snyder Ranch vicinity in McPherson County, Nebraska – Early 1900s

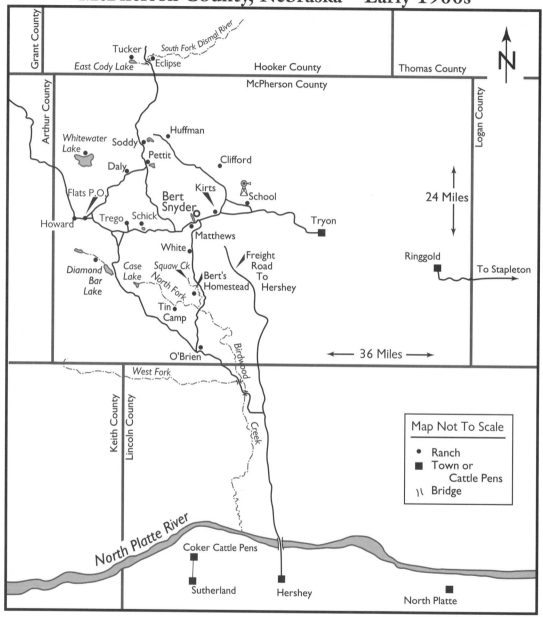

Grant County

South Fork Dismal River

Tucker
East Cody Lake
Eclipse

Hooker County

McPherson County

Thomas County

Logan County

N

Arthur County

Whitewater Lake
Soddy
Huffman
Pettit
Daly
Clifford

Flats P.O.
Bert Snyder
Kirts
School

Howard
Trego
Schick
Tryon

24 Miles

Matthews

White
Ringgold

Diamond Bar Lake
Case Lake
Squaw Ck
North Fork
Bert's Homestead

Freight Road To Hershey

To Stapleton

Tin Camp

36 Miles

O'Brien

Birdwood

West Fork

Keith County
Lincoln County

Creek

Map Not To Scale
• Ranch
■ Town or Cattle Pens
)\ Bridge

North Platte River

Coker Cattle Pens

Sutherland
Hershey
North Platte

Map by Joyce and Jim Snyder

Introduction

This story takes place in the Sandhills of Nebraska on the Ten-Bar Ranch twelve miles west of Tryon. We were six: Dad, Mama, Nellie, the oldest, Miles, fifteen months younger, me (Billie or Bill), five years and six months younger than Miles, and Bertie, two years younger than I.

Miles and his horse, Mustard.

Bertie and me and Mama on horseback.

Dad in his older days on a gentle horse.

*The Snyder Ranch
in the early days.*

Aerial view of how the ranch looks today. (View looking north)

Dad with his first great grandchild, David Yost. This was the last picture ever taken of Dad. It was at Christmas 1956, a month before Dad died.

This is as big as Nellie got.

Miles, Miss Guston and Nellie.

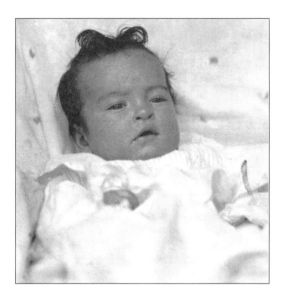

Billie in 1912 - three months old.

Billie in chaps, posing as a cowboy.

Billie's eighth grade graduation photo.

Miles enjoyed his hitch in the army in 1929-30. This picture was taken while he was in Manila.

Chapter One

DON'T FOOL AROUND

As early as I can remember, if my brother Miles wasn't working, he was tinkering. He was always taking something apart and putting it back together again. If possible, Bertie and I were with him. And we were little pests. He put up with us, but he also worked us some.

We didn't mind doing things for Miles. We wanted to be with him and be a part of what he was doing.

When Miles was eleven, Bertie was three and I was five. One of our aunts was up at the ranch visiting. She said, "Miles, why do you make those little girls go get things for you?"

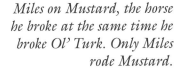
Miles on Mustard, the horse he broke at the same time he broke Ol' Turk. Only Miles rode Mustard.

Miles told her, "If I go and leave them here, my work is all messed up when I get back."

When Miles sent one of us for something, he always added, "Now don't fool around too long." That meant hurry back.

Miles taught Mustard to shake hands.

Many years later Miles had to go into a nursing home here in North Platte. He was eighty-nine years old at the time. His family all lived at the ranch fifty miles away. I lived only a few blocks away so I spent as much time as I possibly could with him.

There were times I wondered if Miles really wanted me there. We didn't talk much. We just sat.

One afternoon I was sitting with Miles in his room. We were watching TV. Eva Connell, the mother of Miles' daughter-in-law, was there in the home, too.

I said, "Miles I'm going across the hall to see Eva."

Miles perked up and said, "Alright, but don't fool around too long."

How I loved hearing that expression once more. I knew then he wanted me with him. He was still my beloved brother.

Miles with his bird dog Fanny.

Chapter Two

Using It All

Back in the old days, people were much more conservative than they are today. It seems to me my folks were more conservative than most. Nothing was wasted at our house. When we butchered a beef, every part of the poor animal was made use of. What we couldn't use, the pigs and chickens enjoyed.

The bones were used in many ways. When Dad built fence, he used a long leg bone to make a "dead-man."

It was not unusual for Bertie and me to go out into the pasture with Dad to watch him work. If he took the wagon, we wanted to go along. Dad didn't mind. If Mama didn't need us at the house, we could go. We were handy to be sent to the wagon for whatever was needed. We learned to distinguish one tool from another at a very young age.

The thing that stands out in my mind is the first time I saw Dad build a fence and set a corner post. He sent me to the wagon to bring him "that long cow leg bone."

When I returned with the bone, I asked Dad, "What are you going to do with that?"

Kids weren't supposed to ask too many questions, but that was an all right question and he answered it readily. He said, "I'm going to make a dead-man."

Even I knew that to make a dead man you had to kill him. I knew my dad had never killed anyone and never would. But I also knew he was going to show me how to make a dead man.

I stood there watching as he fastened a piece of barbed wire around the top part of the corner fence post, leaving a few feet of wire on the ground. He wrapped and fastened the end of the wire on the ground around the leg bone.

Next he picked up his spade and dug a deep hole a foot or two feet out from the post. He put the bone into the ground and filled in the hole, leaving the wire from the post to the ground stretched tight. That was a dead-man.

Dead-mans were also used where the fence ended for a gate. The gate was never as tight as the rest of the fence. There had to be something there to hold the fence cattle-tight.

Now back to making use of all the butchered beef and carcass. On the back leg of a beef, below the knee going to the heel, is a piece of very tough meat. That is where we got our dried beef every year. That piece of meat was cut off, soaked in very spicy brine for many days and hung up in the attic by the chimney to dry. It seemed it took that meat forever to dry.

When it was finally ready to eat, we brought a hunk of it down to the kitchen. It was kept in a special place in the cupboard. Whoever wanted to eat dried beef was welcome to cut off as much as he or she wanted.

That meat was the best ever, but was very hard to slice. There was a rule. Each one cut her own. When Bertie and I were out playing and decided we wanted some dried beef, we went into the kitchen, got a sharp knife and cut until our hands got so tired we quit.

One day I can't seem to forget. Bertie and I had gone in and each cut ourselves a hand full of dried beef. Before Bertie got all of her beef eaten, she had to go to the privy. Mama had told

Miles and Dad butchering a heifer.

us never to take food into the privy. She said for one of us to stay outside and hold the food while the other went in. This we always did.

I held Bertie's beef while she went inside. I had already eaten all of my meat so I ate hers while she was in there. That was the meanest trick I ever pulled on my little sister.

We butchered at least one hog each winter. Bertie and I didn't look forward to hog butchering day as much as we did to butchering the beef. The kitchen smelled awful as Mama rendered the lard.

Mama used the lard for frying grease and as shortening in her baking. She kept one large kettle full of lard for fryingcake doughnuts. Miles loved them. She made them often, always two batches—one for Miles and one for the rest of us.

Then there was the sausage. Helping make the sausage was work for Bertie and me.

Some people cleaned out the hog intestines real good and stuffed the sausage into them. We did that one year, but Mama decided it was too much work. She had material that she cut into long strips. She sewed it into long tubes, closed at one end. The open end was placed on the sausage stuffer.

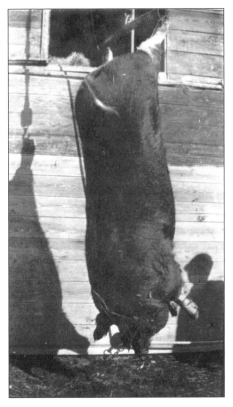

Our porker from which we rendered over nineteen gallons of lard. She was as long as the barn door.

Bertie, Miles or I turned the handle that ground up the pig meat and stuffed the tube Mama had made. (Mama had already added the correct amount of sausage spices to the meat.)

Mama fried some of the sausage into little round patties and packed them down into a large jar of lard. They kept until summer. I don't know if that is what they call summer sausage or not.

Hog butchering wasn't all work for us kids. A hog's dead body was pulled up on the butchering scaffold, then lowered into a barrel of scalding hot water. It was left long enough to loosen the coarse hair.

The hog was pulled up again and left hanging on the scaffold while Dad and Miles scraped off all the hair, including the hair on the tail. Dad cut the tail off and handed it to either Bertie or me, who were standing very close by.

We ran to the house with the tail and gave it to Mama who opened the oven door and put the pigtail on the rack and closed the door. Bertie and I waited until the pigtail was roasted, then the two of us got to eat it.

Then there was the pig's bladder, a very sturdy organ. Dad carefully saved that for Bertie and me, too.

Mama cleaned the bladder the best she could. Miles took the bladder and put buckshot in it to give it weight.

He secured the opening of the bladder to the tube on the tire pump. He pumped in all the air the bladder would hold and tied it off. Bertie and I had a nice ball that we threw and kicked around until it lost all its air.

We had never heard of a football but that is what we had, a nice football. Mama only let us play with it in the kitchen or outdoors. It still left a little grease here and there.

Here is a story I've heard a few times and I believe it.

Oftentimes there was just the ribcage of an animal left on the prairie. It was from an animal that was killed by lightning and died on the spot or an animal that was sick and died near the ranch buildings and had been dragged out there to avoid the bad odor at home as the dead animal decayed. Only the rib cage was left as the coyotes took the other bones to gnaw the meat off.

There was one such ribcage near a main Sandhill trail that served as the mail route. The man who owned the property used the ribcage for his mailbox. The neighbors who shopped for him in town dropped his order off at the carcass. He did this until he could build himself a watertight mailbox.

Today I have two steer skulls, one on each side of my front door, with the horns still attached. There is no doubt that an old rancher's kid lives here.

Many people use cow skulls as decorations. It is not a gruesome sight. It's a tribute to days gone by.

Billie's husband, Bob pushing snow around in front of their house.
Note the cow skulls on either side of the door.

Chapter Three

MAKING A HAY HAND

I liked horses. I was good at handling them for a kid, even if I was just a girl.

The summer I was nine years old, Dad told me he was going to try me on a mowing machine in the hayfield. He had me climb up on the seat of a John Deere mower. He moved the footrest up to where my feet would reach it.

It was a wonderful feeling to know Dad trusted me enough to let me run a mowing machine. And what fun to watch that footrest being lowered an inch or two each year as I grew. I never did get as big as I felt the day he first measured that footrest.

Dad harnessed and hitched a gentle team to MY mower. I hooked up the tugs, feeling about ten feet tall. I sat on my mower seat holding the reins to my team while Dad hitched up his team.

Dad mowing hay. Note the noseflaps on the horses to keep the biting flies off.

Billie on the left driving a four-horse team while Nellie and her friend pretend to pitch hay.

Dad got on his mower and told me to follow him. When moving a mowing machine and it isn't in gear to cut grass, the sickle is raised off the ground a few inches. We had a ways to go to reach the hayfield. We were traveling with the sickles up. We had one barbed wire gate to go through.

We came to the gate and Dad drove right through. By this time I was feeling so big and important, I wasn't watching closely. I caught the end of my sickle on the dead-man wire. The machine swung to the right. The team stopped. I didn't know what happened.

Dad stopped his team, wrapped his reins tightly around the sickle lever and came back to assess the damage. I'd broken the tongue out of the mower.

Neither one of us mowed hay that day. Dad repaired the tongue. I spent the day feeling very bad. In fact, I felt like a kid that would never amount to anything.

The next morning all the repairs were made. I was ready to try mowing again, this time to really watch for trouble before it happened.

Dad and I started out in the same manner, only I was in front of him. We got through the gate fine and drove to the patch of hay to be mowed. I got lined up just right and was able to lower the cutting bar and say "Giddup" to my team, good ol' Silver Heels and Charlie. I was actually mowing hay. What better could a nine-year-old girl ask for!

Dad waited until I got a ways ahead, then started mowing in behind me. Gee Whiz!!! This was wonderful. I had the best feeling in my chest. I knew that none of the neighbor's boys had started mowing hay as young as I.

Suddenly the mower stopped with a jerk. The good ol' team just stood there waiting to be told what to do. I sure wanted to get this taken care of before Dad got there.

I hopped off my machine and went in front of the sickle to see what I'd hit. Just when I got to where I could see, Dad hollered at me in a very severe voice, "BILL, GET OUT FROM IN FRONT OF THAT SICKLE!"

I did.

It turned out I had hit an anthill big enough to stop the mower. Dad scolded me some more, saying, "Never get in front of a mower sickle while horses are hitched to the machine." He said if something spooked the horses, and they started to run, I could get my feet cut off.

Dad had me back the horses up until the sickle was free of the anthill. I pulled on the lever to lift the sickle high enough to clear the ant nest, said, "Giddup" and mowed over the anthill. I dropped the sickle and was on my way.

I mowed hay every summer for the next five years. I don't recall any more problems. I did do a lot of little girl swearing at my sweet old horses. The horses didn't mind and it made me feel bigger and more important.

Billie driving the stacker team.

Miles on the sweep. Billie is on the right, ready to drive the stacker team.

This might be a good place to tell about the time I hired the hay-hand. I don't remember how old I was, but I know I was old enough to tell a good-looking young man from an older fellow who wasn't so good-looking.

It was getting time to start haying. Dad hadn't found a man to hire to help us. This particular morning Dad and Miles left to ride the pastures. I knew they wouldn't be back until noon.

Shortly after they left, a good-looking, clean, young man drove into our barnyard. I was the only person he saw. He said he had heard we were looking for help in the hay field.

I said we were.

I asked him all the questions I'd heard Dad ask a man before hiring him. I told him we would hire him. I told him what day we would start haying and to come the night before. I told him he'd sleep in the bunkhouse and Mama would do his washing. And I told him we always fed good at our house.

This man had his own car and Dad wouldn't have to go to town to pick him up or take him to town when haying was over. I felt I had done a good job of helping Dad run the ranch. I had a hard time waiting for him to ride in at noon. I was right out there to tell him I had hired our hay hand.

Dad didn't look happy about it, but there was nothing he could do, as there was no way to get in touch with our new hired man.

The new man showed up on time. I don't even remember his name. Dad put him to work. He was a good worker and had worked in hayfields before. Everything went along great for a few days until that good-looking young man with a car took my older sister, Nellie, for a ride one evening. Dad fired him the next day.

He replaced him with an older man without a car. I guess Dad didn't mind picking up the hired man and taking him back when his job run out.

I never hired any more men for Dad.

Chapter Four

DAD AND MAMA GO ON A TRIP

Dad and Mama had been married twenty-three years. All twenty-three years had been spent on the ranch. They now had four kids: Nellie, twenty, Miles, nineteen, Billie, fourteen and Bertie, twelve.

In the spring of 1926 Dad and Mama decided to take a trip. I don't remember it being called a vacation. If someone took a few days off and left home, they went on a trip. The only vacations we knew about were the two weeks off from school at Christmas time.

Dad and Mama had planned this trip during the winter with our good friends and neighbors, Bird and Ruby Huffman. They were going to the Black Hills in South Dakota. Early summer, well before haying time, they packed their camping gear and left.

Their two full-grown kids, along with their two half-grown kids, were well able to take care of the ranch for a few days.

Dad, Bird and Mama under a big red rock near Devil's Tower.

Unsuspecting Mama, Dad, Ruby and Bird Huffman in front of a lodge in the Black Hills of South Dakota.

I don't remember how long they were to be gone. It seemed like forever to the Saturday night before they were to get home.

Nellie had a boyfriend named Shorty Varner. Come Saturday night, Nellie and Shorty had a date to go to a dance in Arthur, a small town twenty sandy miles northwest of our home.

Bertie and I wanted to go to the dance with Nellie. This was something we knew the folks would never allow, but the folks weren't there to stop us and it was hard for Nellie to say no to her little sisters. Bertie and I hurried and washed our hands and faces, pulled on our good dresses and pulled on our shoes.

Shorty had an old Ford Roadster. Cars were narrow in those days, but there was no law to tell how many could ride in one seat. We were all little, including Shorty.

Ruby, Bird and Dad near the Devil's Tower.

We all four piled into Shorty's Roadster. Shorty was driving. Nellie sat next to Shorty. I sat next to Nellie with Bertie on my lap.

We had to leave well before dark to get to the dance by the time it started. I don't remember helping with the milking. We must have left it all for Miles. Miles had been trusted to take care of the ranch while the folks were gone. He would do nothing to break that trust. But we three girls saw a chance to get away with something. We were feeling very grown up. The folks not being there was great.

We were sailing along about ten miles an hour when Nellie asked Shorty to let her drive. He readily did so. They exchanged places and Shorty showed Nellie what you do to a Model T Ford to get it going. She was soon doing just fine on a nice piece of straight road at about fifteen miles an hour.

The road made a sharp turn to the left. Nellie went straight on. She hit a bump as the car left the road. We came to a sudden stop.

Miles, the good brother who stayed at home while his sisters went catting, and Shorty Varner, Nellie's boyfriend.

Bertie was the only one hurt. She was on my lap with her face close to the windshield. The left side of her head hit and broke the windshield, cutting her face all around her eye. I guess the reason God put eyes into sockets was to protect them.

We were in a mess. Bertie was bleeding all over us, the folks were a long way off and we shouldn't even have been where we were.

I don't remember how badly the windshield was broken, but Shorty was able to get the car back on the road. We were much closer to Arthur than we were to home. We drove on into Arthur.

Arthur did not have a doctor but they did have a little drug store that was still open. We took Bertie there and someone cleaned her up and put plenty of gauze on her face. They tried to tape the deep cuts together.

By now it was way after dark and we had forgotten all about the dance. All we wanted was to get home, but that would take at least two hours. Travel on Sandhill roads after dark is slower than in the daylight. This was due to twisty roads and the dim lights on the old Fords. We did get home and sneaked up to bed without waking Miles.

Poor Shorty didn't have much of a Saturday night on his date with Nellie.

The next morning Bertie's face looked much worse. It was badly swollen and discolored. (I'm sure she didn't have to help with the milking.) The folks were due home that night. How we dreaded their arrival.

Late that afternoon Mama and Dad came driving in, anxious to see their kids. Three of those kids met the car with guilt showing all over their faces.

After all was explained, Dad said, "The first time in all these years Mom and I take a trip and you pull something like this." He scolded Nellie pretty good, also saying, "Bertie will have scars on her face all her life."

At eighty-nine years old, Bertie still does have scars to remind us of what we did when we knew better. Of course, if the folks had been there, they could have taken her to North Platte. A doctor might have stitched her face up. But that is a lot of hindsight. On second thought, if the folks had been there, this wouldn't have happened.

A neighbor told the folks that "sweet-oil" would help the cuts to heal, leaving less scaring. The next mail day, Mama had Charlie Coker bring up a bottle of "sweet-oil." Bertie faithfully rubbed it on her cuts until the bottle was empty. She still wound up with scars, just like Dad said.

All of the people in the Sandhills knew what the three Snyder girls did while their parents went on a trip to the Black Hills. I don't believe Nellie ever had another date with Shorty. After all, he had to replace that windshield.

Chapter Five

MAKING DO

Living fifty miles from town out in the Sandhills, everyone made do. Those fifty miles of roads were sandy trails made in earlier days by lumber wagons. Since the landscape was all sandhills to the Platte River Valley, five miles north of North Platte, the roads were all through sand.

The trail, we'll call it, went up one hill and down the next with somewhat level ground between (sometimes). Even the level trail had some twists in it before you reached the next hill.

Driving an old Model T Ford, it was hard to get up any speed. Speed was what you needed to make it up those sandy hills without getting stuck. If the hills were spaced right, the driver could use the speed he gained coming down one hill to make it up the next, that is, if the stretch between the hills was straight.

If the car slowed to a certain speed going uphill, everyone but the driver jumped out, ran around behind, put their shoulders against the car and pushed with all their might. If the car made it to the top of the hill, the pushers and the car arrived at the same time. The pushers climbed back into their places and the car was on its way.

If the pushers' help was not enough to get the car to the top of the hill, the driver backed down as far as he thought necessary and took another run. The pushers stood on the spot where the car had started to back down.

With the load lightened, expert driving and a little luck, the car made it all the way to the top. When that happened, the pushers raced up the hill after the car and climbed back into their places.

If the car slowed to an almost stop before reaching the top, the pushers rushed in behind and again pushed for all they were worth. At the top, everyone crawled in and was usually somewhat rested by the time they reached the next hill where they again had to get out and push.

Some of the time all the driver had to do when coming to a hill was push the clutch in, putting the Ford in low gear, and pull the gas lever as far down as possible. The gas lever was very handy. It was placed just behind the steering wheel. The driver could easily reach it with the fingers of his right hand. (The lever that controlled the spark was behind the steering wheel on the left side.) The driver gave the old car all the gas he could, thus making it over the hill without a shove.

The trips to town were few and far between. We made do. We never threw anything away. As Dad always told us, "Now save that. You might have a use for it some day."

We saved everything. All things we bought at a store were wrapped in paper and tied with string. We saved the paper and we saved the string. It was fun to watch that ball of string grow. When we had to wrap a package to mail, we were always able to find a piece of wrapping paper the right size and we always had plenty of string.

The only paper sacks I remember were the ones the hard candy came in. They were very small, but they were sacks. We saved them, too.

The groceries were packed in wooden boxes. Those wooden boxes came in very handy. They were used as cupboards in the bunkhouse, the washhouse and the meathouse. We even used them upstairs in the kids' bedrooms and in the hall between our rooms. When we wanted to be decorative, we tacked a pretty piece of material on the front of the box.

The best boxes were the ones about three feet long with a dividing board in the center. Stand one of those on end and you had the start of a real cupboard.

Bertie and Me and Miles Too

Ruth Thornburg, Billie's mother-in-law, and her Model T.

The east door off our kitchen led into a room the width of the kitchen. We called it the storeroom. In it was kept the year's supplies Dad freighted out each fall from a town down on the railroad. When Dad finished the freighting, that storeroom had at least a dozen fifty-pound sacks of flour (Mama baked lots of bread) and a couple of hundred-pound sacks of sugar.

There was always one of those long wooden boxes full of soda crackers. The crackers were in layers. Soda crackers in the good old days were over twice the size of the crackers we get now in little red or blue paper boxes. They may not have been as tasty as the ones we have now, but they sure were good in potato or tomato soup or in oyster stew.

I have a memory that is funny now, but at the time, I thought it made a lot of sense. The flour sacks were a perfect size for dishtowels. As each flour sack became empty, Mama bleached out the lettering and whatever advertising picture was on the sack. She did this by boiling the sack in strong, soapy water. Then she stenciled another picture, a bird or a flower, and embroidered the new design with colored floss. She hemmed the sack and had a fancy dishtowel.

The time I remember, the sack had a picture of a red bull on the front. I thought that picture was so pretty. I asked Mama to leave the bull's picture and embroider around that. Mama just laughed at me and went to all the work of boiling out the bull and putting a bird's picture in his place.

When the dishtowels were worn out, they went into the rag box to make our next living room rug.

The storeroom also served as a spare bedroom. The double bed in there was always made and ready to be crawled into. Our neighbors all knew of our spare bedroom. It was not unusual for one of them to be late getting home and going by our place on horseback after our lamps were out. He would stop, put his horse in the barn, unsaddle him and give him hay. He then quietly came into our house, went into the storeroom and went to bed. Our loving old black and white Australian shepherd dog knew all the neighbors and would make no sound.

The storeroom also served as the Lilac Post Office. The U.S. Government furnished a three-foot tall wooden box with a dozen pigeonholes. The Downings, the Fairchilds, the Kirts and the Snyders received mail from the Lilac Post Office and each had a pigeonhole, which meant three pigeonholes were needed for the mail. Mama was postmistress so the Snyders did not need a pigeonhole. Mama kept personal things in the other nine little boxes.

There was a big scale on the floor of the storeroom. It also belonged to the U.S. Government. It weighed anything up to one hundred pounds.

How the mail came thirty miles from Sutherland when the weather was bad. Here's Charlie Coker, the mailman, making a winter delivery.

Bertie and Me and Miles Too

We kids soon learned to weigh ourselves. It was fun to stand on the scales and push the little weights along to see if we had gotten any bigger. I remember how wonderful it felt the day I stepped on the scales and weighed one hundred pounds. I felt very grown up. That storeroom was the most interesting place in the house, except for the shelf in Mama's closet where she hid things from Bertie and me.

What a Needle Can Do
By Mrs. A. B. Snyder (Mama)

(Read at the Flats Helping Hand Meeting and then published in the
"Tryon Graphic" in 1943)

I want to tell you
What a needle can do
With the help of scissors
A thimble and you,
And, as my imagination strayed,
Here are some of the things
That I've seen made.

The snow white cloth
From sacks of flour
Made lovely gifts
For the bridal shower.

Miles' old blue pants
Tho long and slim,
Made a very nice pair
Of pants for Jim.

Jack's old plaid shirt
That was once so smart
Turned good side out
Made a jacket for Art.

From Riley's duck trousers
And two feed sacks
Edna made Barbara
A suit of slacks.

Don's old wedding pants
That hung 'neath the stair,
Furnished the cloth
For Merlyn a pair.

Helen's pretty silk dress
For a year or so,
Now goes to school
As a blouse for Jo.

From old white blankets
That come in soft pairs
Margie made Morris
A number of squares.

A cigarette burn
Had spoiled a new shirt,
So Opal made Peggy
A suspender skirt.

From a pair of Glenn's pants
With a long leg rip
Grandma made a pair
For little boy Skip.

Carol's pretty pink jumper
And silk pin-a-fore
Was once a dress
That her mother wore.

The pretty colored felt
From a laid-away hat
Cecil even made baby's
Shoes from that.

From Wayne's big red jacket
With frayed collars and cuffs
Eva's two little girls
Wear leggins and muffs.

We have mended our hose
And darned our socks
So that they, too, can take
A few more knocks.

And many more things
For Sissie and Bub
Have been made from old cloth
By the Helping Hand Club.

There are some I know
Who always frown
On a garment they think
Is a "hand-me-down."

But think of the cloth
This needle saves
To make natty uniforms
For the WAACS and WAVES.

And the money we've saved
If invested in bonds,
Will buy guns for our boys
Far across the ponds.

There is no end
To what a needle can do
With scissors and thimble
And help from you.

Chapter Six

MILES' GOLD WATCH

When Miles was three months old, Mama went "down home" to Cozad to visit her family for Christmas and to show off her baby boy. In Mama's family, the McCance's, there were seven girls and only two boys. Boys were rare and very special in that family.

While she was there, Miles came down with pneumonia and was very, very sick. By some miracle, Baby Miles recovered in spite of the doctor's treatment. I can still see Mama shaking her head as she tells the story of the doctor insisting that they keep the air in the house as dry as possible. Above all, "don't hang any washed clothes up to dry in the house." In was into January and the coldest part of the year when Miles got sick and people dried the washed clothes in the house by the fire at that time.

Nellie was only fifteen months older than Miles, so Mama had two babies in diapers. Each diaper had to be washed and dried before it was put back on the baby. It would be sixty or seventy years before there were throw-away diapers. Mama is gone now and I can't ask her how she managed, but I know it was rough. It was several weeks before Mama was able to return to the ranch with the two babies.

When the doctor released Miles, he told Mama the pneumonia had damaged Miles' lungs and heart and he should never smoke. While Miles was still very young, Mama promised she would buy him a gold watch if he didn't smoke. It worked. Miles never smoked and he got his gold watch on his twenty-first birthday.

In the early nineteen hundreds, a gold watch was the ultimate in a timepiece. There were dollar watches and many kinds of cheap watches. A gold pocket watch was the envy of most every man. I remember Miles' watch had a very pretty face and was in a gold case. A cover snapped shut over the glass face. It also had a gold chain and was usually worn in a vest pocket.

Wristwatches for men came out in the early nineteen twenties, but men didn't like wearing them for fear of being branded as a "sissy." Women and girls were crazy about wristwatches.

Dad thought a watch was an unnecessary item to own and carry around. He told time by the sun and very accurately. Mama had dinner ready at noon sharp, and Dad always had the hay crew in and ready to sit down at the table at that time. Dad never owned a watch.

The only other timepiece on the ranch was the big kitchen clock that sat on a wall shelf behind the long dining table. This faithful old clock struck every hour, one dong for each hour, one through twelve. On half-past, the clock struck one dong. If you heard it strike a dong at night, you wondered what hour it was half-past.

Every seven days Mama had to go to the clock, open the glass door, take the key off the shelf and wind the clock.

Miles and Mama. Miles was very proud of the gauntlets he is wearing on his arm.

Bertie and Me and Miles Too

To clean the big clock, Mama took it off the shelf, set it on the kitchen table, opened the back and brushed all the works with a turkey feather she had dipped in kerosene. Wish I knew where that old clock was today.

Miles' watch disappeared. His son, Jim, says he remembers when the watch stopped working. He went with his dad to take the watch into a jewelry store to be repaired. He was also with him several times when he returned to the shop to pick up the watch. Each time the jeweler told Miles it wasn't ready. The last time he went in after it, the jeweler told him they had sent it away for repairs and it had never been returned.

The whole family felt bad about Miles losing that watch. We all believed it was such a wonderful watch that it was stolen.

Dad's timepiece is still in the sky and if he were here, he'd still be using it to tell the time of day.

Chapter Seven

DIPPED IN A HORSE TANK

As a kid, three or four years old, the horse tank was the most fascinating thing on the ranch. As the saying goes, I must have been about knee-high to a grasshopper at the time. I remember reaching over the edge of the tank and dangling my fingers in the water and watching the water ripple away. I also remember being told to stay away from the tank, even being scolded and told that I might fall in the tank and drown. I did not understand what drowning was. I just knew it was something I was not supposed to do and if I fell into the horse tank, I would do it. I was forever trying to slip up to the horse tank without being caught.

One evening, Mama, Dad and Miles were in the corral, milking. I was out there watching what everyone was doing and managed to get over to the tank with no one seeing me, or so I thought. I was standing there dangling my hands in the water and wondering how in the

Bertie and Nibs checking a windmill and tank.

world I could fall in. The rim of the tank came up high on my chest, which was about two feet off the ground. As I was thinking there was no way I could fall in the tank just standing there, my feet came off the ground and my head went straight down into the tank.

Just as quickly, I was out of the tank with my feet on the ground.

Mama was standing behind me, laughing. Dad and Miles were laughing. I thought they were laughing at me for not minding and falling into the tank. I could tell Mama had pulled me out. I was dripping wet, all but my shoes. Thinking back on this, I realize Mama slipped up behind me, grabbed my feet and upended me in the tank to teach me a lesson.

For years I couldn't ride past a horse tank and windmill. If the windmill was running, I went out of my way to get to it, get off my horse and drink the wonderful cold water, even if I wasn't thirsty. If there was more than one horsebacker, we all did the same thing.

I was short and had to stretch myself out on the pipe to reach the stream of water. It took practice to do this without getting water up my nose, but it was fun and tasted so good on a hot day. We each wiped our mouths with the backs of our hand, got back on our horses and rode on.

It was a big disappointment to be out horseback on a hot day and heading over a hill on a fast trot to where we knew there was a tank and windmill, anticipating a drink of good, cold water, only to notice as we got closer that the wheel wasn't turning. There wasn't enough wind. No cold water! Then we were really thirsty. It was no use trying another windmill as there wasn't any wind to turn them either.

Neighbors and friends at a get-together at our house. The tank Billie was dipped in is in the background.

Another horse tank.

Our thirsty horses, of course, would take a drink out of the tank. We never got that thirsty.

Another thing we were not allowed to do was climb the windmill, get on the wheel platform and turn the wheel by hand to try to get some water. Dad said that if the wind should change directions, the wheel could swing around and knock us off the platform. We would land in the tank and drown.

By this time I knew what drowning was and saw the possibility of what Dad said. Besides, I had learned to mind the folks even if they were a few miles away.

I'm still fascinated with horse tanks and windmills.

Chapter Eight

HOME REMEDIES

Illnesses, accidents and ailments, Mama had a remedy for every misery any of us might have. None of them were too bad but the castor oil. THAT Bertie and I refused to swallow. Mama and Dad had a system for trying to make us take it. Dad would stand behind one of us holding our hands and arms flat against our chest while Mama poked a spoonful of castor oil into our mouth. The recipient would spit the stuff out.

This one I'll hand to Bertie. She was the one getting the dose of castor oil. Dad had a good grip on her. Mama stuck a spoonful of the nasty stuff into her mouth. Bertie immediately turned her head and rubbed her open mouth the full length of Dad's shirtsleeve, from his elbow over his bare hand. I recall Dad saying, "We won't do that again."

It was the last time the folks ever tried to give us castor oil. It was supposed to make kids healthy, but they decided we just might live and grow up without it.

Not too long after that, the family was visiting relatives in Maxwell. Bertie and I wanted to stay all night with our two cousins, Nellie and Eddy Sullivan. Dad and Mama were spending the night at Uncle John's, a few miles out in the country.

Bertie and I were having a fine time until it came bedtime. Aunt Pearl brought out the castor oil bottle and a big tablespoon. Nellie and Eddy went right up to her. Bertie and I backed off.

Grandpa Snyder with my cousins Nellie and Eddie Sullivan.

Aunt Pearl said, "Everyone has to take a dose of castor oil at my house."

We explained that the folks didn't give us the stuff any more, but she made us take it and we had to swallow it. Bertie and I never stayed all night with Nellie and Eddy again.

A remedy I liked was the one we had for chilblains. Bertie and I rode five miles horseback to school, which was fine in nice weather. During the dead of winter (sometimes it seemed to be the dead of winter most all winter), we got chilblains. Even though we wore heavy stockings and heavy overshoes over our shoes, our feet got cold enough to cause chilblains. Our heels stung and itched something fierce.

Mama's way of doctoring chilbains was to have us rub raw onions on our heels. I have a picture in my head of Bertie and me sitting by the living room heater with our shoes and stockings off, our long underwear legs rolled up. Mama cut an onion in two, giving Bertie and me each a half. We sat there and rubbed onion on first one heel and then the other.

Mama on Snip. Mama was on her way to help a sick neighbor. In a sack on the saddle is a jar of chicken soup.

My problem was that I loved the taste of onions. My mouth watered all the time I was doing it. The first time we did it, I asked Mama if I could eat my half of the onion when I finished.

Mama said, "No."

I don't know if all this helped our chilblains but it gave us something to do and delayed our going upstairs to bed.

Another remedy I remember plainly was the one for Summer Complaint. Summer Complaint was a very bad diarrhea that only hit in the hot summer months and then only babies and small kids got it. Bertie was plagued with it.

A certain little weed grew in the pastures that cured Summer Complaint. All Mama had to do was send Dad out in the pasture to search until he found enough of the weed to boil to make a drink of tea. One drink was all it took to cure Summer Complaint. I wish I knew the name of the tiny weed. It grew flat on the ground and had wee little red leaves. It was hard to find among the taller pasture grasses.

Now we come to Dad's remedies. He had two: kerosene and whiskey. When he felt a sore throat coming on, he got the kerosene can, tipped his head way back and poured a little kerosene into his throat. He then gargled and spit it out, making an awful face. He wanted the rest of us to try it, but we preferred the greased wool rag that Mama wrapped around our neck when our throats got sore.

Hot toddies were also medicine, but Dad was the only one that doctored with those. I don't remember what had to be wrong with Dad for him to need a hot toddy.

The one time Dad doctored Mama is plain in my mind. The year was 1919. Mama was in bed and very sick. The closest doctor was thirty-five miles and several hours away. Dad talked Mama into trying a hot toddy.

Mama drank the hot toddy Dad fixed for her. Bertie and I stood by and watched. We watched everything we were allowed to. Mama had never tasted whiskey before and she made an awful face. We all waited awhile, but it didn't make her well.

Dad with Towser

Dad gave her another one, one that he no doubt made a little stronger.

Dad went out to the living room. I was in the bedroom by Mama's bed waiting for her to feel better. Suddenly Mama yelled in a terrifying voice, "BERT, I'M DYING."

Dad came hurrying into the bedroom. Mama convinced him she was really dying. Dad rushed back to the living room and grabbed the receiver off the hook. He gave Central a fast ring and called Dr. Saddler in Hershey.

By the time the doctor arrived in the late afternoon, the effect of the hot toddies had worn off. Mama's bed had quit whirling but she was still plenty sick. Little Bertie had gotten sick, too, and crawled into bed with Mama.

Dr. Saddler took one look at them and said they had the flu and the rest of us would get it. He left enough pills for the whole family and headed back to Hershey. The pills were free, but doctors charged one dollar per mile when making house calls out in the country.

Dr. Sadler had spent all day coming to our ranch, doctoring Mama and Bertie and getting back home. Mama told Dad giving her those hot toddies and getting her drunk cost him thirty-five dollars.

Mama never drank another hot toddy, but Dad cured himself many times with his own home remedy. Mama had made a bad face when she drank her hot toddy, but Dad always let out a great, big, satisfying, "AAAAH," as he drank his.

Mama used to have terrible headaches. She called them sick headaches. Now they are called migraine headaches. The only thing Mama had to take for those awful migraines was Bromo Seltzer.

The Bromo Seltzer came in a pretty, dark blue bottle. It was a large, white granule that was dissolved in a glass of water. You had to drink it down fast before it stopped fizzing.

Bertie and I were usually at Mama's side to watch her drink her Bromo Seltzer. She always made an awful face as she drank it. I picked up the empty glass once and tasted it. I thought it tasted good and was always hoping Mama would leave a little in the glass and I could taste it before the bite got out of the fizz. The Bromo Seltzer did not stop the headaches. Mama just had to "tuffy" them out.

The only other doctoring that Mama did was take Carters Little Liver Pills. I don't know what she took them for or what they were supposed to do for her. I don't think they even make Carters Little Liver Pills any more.

There was one time that made me a little special. I stepped on a nail. I don't remember my foot hurting, but the folks were worried and gave me lots of attention.

Mama told me to go soak my foot in hot salt water. Dad made me a crutches out of a stick that was kind of round and kind of wasn't, but looked like it would make a good pair of kid crutches.

Mama and Dad in their later years. They both survived each other's home remedies.

Dad measured me. Then he cut two long lengths from the stick and two shorter pieces, each about three inches long. He nailed one short piece on the end of each of the longer sticks.

I was so pleased with those crutches. I kept my foot sore as long as I could.

Bertie saw all the attention I was getting. After I finally discarded the crutches, she convinced the folks she had a mighty sore foot. She started walking on the crutches and got by with it until Dad caught her holding up the wrong foot as she hobbled along.

Chapter Nine

THE TALKING MACHINE

I don't know how it came about. Nellie was home that summer and she may have had something to do with the folks' decision. Anyway, Mama and Dad told us we could have a Talking Machine. The real name for it was phonograph, but we called it the Talking Machine.

Nellie brought a Monkey Wards Catalog to Mama and we picked out the Talking Machine we wanted. It was a big one, not the kind that had to be set on a table.

We still had to get Dad's ok. When we showed the picture and the price to him, he said, "Go ahead."

Mama made out the order and it went out on that day's mail.

Our mail came twice a week from Sutherland, thirty-five miles south of the ranch. Charley Coker carried the mail in an old Ford Runabout with a box on the back. Charley carried freight as well as the U.S. mail, that is, if it was small enough to go in a little pickup. Mama said it would be at least two weeks before we could start looking for our Talking Machine.

We counted the days until two weeks were up. From then on, each Tuesday and Saturday, Nellie, Bertie and I stood out in the yard south of the house where we had a good view of the road where Charlie and his Runabout would be bouncing along.

The day we saw Charlie come into view and we saw that tall crate in the box on his Ford, I remember Nellie jumping up and down yelling, "Here it comes."

We three ran from the south yard, through the house and out to the barn where Charlie always parked. It was noon, "dinner time," and the men were at the barn just ready to come to the house to eat. They helped Charlie untie and unload the Talking Machine. They carried it to the house, carefully uncrated it and carried it into the living room.

Mama was postmistress of the Lilac Post Office. She had to feed Charlie his dinner and get the mail ready to go back to Sutherland. Nellie and Miles read the instructions. Dad stood back watching.

I could barely see in when they raised the lid. Bertie had to climb up on a chair to see what was in there. Under the lid was a turntable with a thing beside it that we could swing over the turntable. The directions told us to select a record and place it on the turntable.

There were some Talking Machine needles in a little box, some of the needles were thick and some were thin. The directions said: Use a thick needle if you want it to play loud; use a thin needle if you want it to play soft. That was the only way to control the volume.

There was a crank right handy on the outside of the machine. The directions told us to turn the crank until the spring was wound up. The crank started to turn harder as the spring got wound up. If we wound it too tight, the spring would break so we had to be careful. Next we moved the little lever at the side of the turntable to "on." The record started turning. We set the needle on the record and the machine started talking.

We all stood there waiting for that first word. WHAT A THRILL! That first word was "Hello."

The name of the record was "Cohen on the Telephone." It was a one-sided conversation of an old man talking on the telephone for the first time. He was having a hard time understanding what the other fellow was saying. The other fellow was having a hard time hearing and understanding Cohen. We all thought it was so funny. We played it over and over.

Every time a neighbor came in or we had company, one of us kids played "Cohen on the Telephone" for them, that is, if Mama would let us. We always had to ask Mama if we could play the Talking Machine. I'm sure there were times Mama said no and the lucky visitor was spared the ordeal of Bertie and me explaining all the funny parts to them.

As the Talking Machine played, Bertie and I stood right there watching the turntable go round and round, Bertie on the chair she pulled up and me stretching my full height so I could see in and reach the needle and move it back.

We soon caught on to picking up the needle as soon as it played a funny part and setting it back a little so it would play the funny stuff over again. We always did that as we played it for company, just in case they didn't get it all the first time. Bertie and I became quite the operators. Bertie says I got to play more records than she did, but I don't remember it that way.

Other records came with the machine, but I don't remember them. Most of them were talking records. Each time we put on a new record, we had to wind it up again. If we didn't, about the middle of the next record, the turntable would slow down and the words would be drawn out as though the talker was slowly dying. We thought that was funny, too.

The Talking Machine needles would get dull, making it hard on the record to use them. One time we ran out of sharp needles. We were told not to play the machine until we could get to town and get new needles. We missed playing our Talking Machine.

One day brother Miles came in from the pasture with some long, strong stickers from a cactus. He put one in the slot for the needle, tightened the screw, cranked, turned the machine on and placed the cactus needle on the record. It played soft and clear.

Miles stood there with his happy one-sided grin on his face. He had made a great discovery. Look at the money we could save on Talking Machine needles.

As the record finished playing, the cactus needle was worn out. But that was ok. We just went out in the pasture and got lots of needles.

There is a sad memory connected with the Talking Machine. We got our Talking Machine in late summer.

Each fall, many duck hunters came to our ranch as soon as duck season opened. Our lakes were great places for duck hunting. The same hunters came each year and put up nice big tents in our barnyard. They camped there three or four days.

Bertie and I loved this. We would hurry home from school when the hunters were there. They always gave us lots of attention. Come Christmastime, they always sent Bertie and me something very nice.

The year we got our Talking Machine, Bertie and I took each group of hunters into the house and showed them our wonderful machine that talked. That Christmas a gift from one group of duck hunters was several records for our Talking Machine. These records were all music, Hawaiian music.

Here is the sad part.

A short time before Christmas, Dad and Miles butchered a beef. While skinning the beef, Dad got a cut on the pointing finger of his right hand. The cut did not heal. He soon got infection, which turned into blood poisoning. Blood poisoning was a very scary word in the early nineteen hundreds before antibiotics.

Dad's finger swelled and turned black. Then his hand started swelling and turning dark. Mama and Dad used all of the home remedies they knew. It still grew worse. Dad was feeling sick all over.

They called Dr. McGraw from Tryon. Dr. McGraw, who weighed less than a hundred pounds, and her one-armed husband, Joe, who was her driver, served the Sandhills faithfully and well for many years. Dr. McGraw had the reputation of never refusing a call.

Dr. McGraw came right out, that is, she started right out as soon as she got our phone call. With the twelve miles of sandy, hilly roads and Joe's one-arm driving, it took an hour to reach the ranch.

Everyone in the Sandhills loved Dr. McGraw. She would cuss and use baby talk in the same sentence. I plainly remember Mama whispering to Bertie and me that she was afraid that Daddy's hand was paining him so much he might use some cuss words in front of the lady doctor.

By the time Dr. McGraw got finished examining Daddy, Mama realized the little lady doctor could handle her patient *and* his cussing from pain.

When Dr. McGraw left, she and Joe had our Daddy with them, taking him to the hospital in North Platte. She told us it was blood poisoning. Daddy had a five-hour ride over rough, twisty, Sandhill roads to reach North Platte.

It was in late December and the days were short. It was far after dark when they reached the Platte Valley Hospital, an old two-story building. There were ten rooms for patients, all double rooms. There was one full bath on the first floor and one toilet on the second floor.

The North Platte doctor kept Daddy in the hospital. Dr. McGraw and Joe headed back to Tryon. Very early the next morning our phone rang. Mama got up to answer it. Dr. McGraw told Mama they had to keep Daddy in the hospital. His hand was very bad. They might have to take it off.

That very evening was Christmas Eve. Our family always celebrated Christmas by opening our presents on Christmas Eve.

We did the chores early and had an early supper of potato soup. A very quiet, sad family opened gifts that evening. We had heard nothing more from the hospital during the day.

We played the records the Duck Hunters had sent us for a gift. We all thought the music was beautiful, but it kind of had a sad sound.

While we were listening to this beautiful, sad music, the phone rang. Mama answered it. It was the hospital calling to tell us they had just amputated Daddy's finger and might have to take the whole hand off by morning.

Daddy's hand got well and all he lost was the first half of his index finger of his right hand. It was several days before Dr. McGraw brought him home, sweet-talking the Poor Dear in every breath.

It was so good to have him home.

Dad said he'd had to have someone else write the check for his hospital bill, including the signature. He'd only put an "x" by his name. He had us all get pencil and paper and practice writing our name with our left hand.

The next few days Bertie and I had fun trying to see who could do the best job. We never did learn to write left-handed. We are still as right-handed as ever.

And to this day, eighty years later, I can't listen to Hawaiian music and not think of that Christmas Eve back on the ranch.

Chapter Ten

AFRAID OF THE DARK

Bertie and I were both afraid in the dark. We called it being afraid of the dark. We were only afraid if we were alone. I remember Dad telling a story about a time I was a two-year-old kid and had fallen asleep lying on the sette.

The rest of the family were ready to go to bed and had blown out the light. The moon was shining through the window. It lit up the seat of the chair Mama had put by the settee to keep me from falling off. Dad came over to carry the sleeping me upstairs and put me in bed with my sister Nellie.

As Dad moved the chair to pick me up, I went into a frightened crying spell. When the folks got me quieted down enough to tell them what was the matter, I told them I had seen the dark jump off the chair. As Dad had moved the chair, the moon reflection went from the seat onto the floor. Dad loved to tease me by telling that story.

Bertie and I had a rule. If one of us had to go anyplace that was dark, the other one had to go with her. This wasn't a problem during the summer. We were in bed by the time it was dark.

During the winter, it was cold and dark early. If one of us had to go to the privy, the other one had to go along. It seemed to me Bertie had to go a lot more often than I did, which, of course, wasn't fair. (We were always arguing over what was or wasn't fair.)

Billie and Bertie. Where one went, the other had to go.

One winter after supper, the family moved into the living room to spend the long evening doing his or her thing. The lamp had been moved into the living room and the door to the kitchen had been closed to conserve heat. The kitchen was dark.

The bucket with our drinking water was on the washstand far across the kitchen from the living room door. Whoever went for a drink of water left the door open, but made a fast trip so not to cool off the living room. Of course, when Bertie or I went after a drink, we hurried, as even with the light from the living room, it was quite dark in that corner.

One evening Bertie had a bad case of hiccups. She kept saying, "Somebody scare me so I can get rid of these hiccups." No one tried to scare her.

She went to the kitchen for a drink of water, hoping that might do the trick. I had a wonderful idea. As Bertie reached the water bucket, I closed the door.

Bertie ran back across the kitchen, jerked the door open and said, "Mama, Bill closed the door on me."

Somehow I had a feeling I wouldn't be scolded.

Mama let Bertie stand there for a few seconds then said, "Where are your hiccups?"

I sure got away with that one.

Chapter Eleven

OLD SAYINGS

Expressions the folks used in the old days sound funny to me now. Dad seemed to judge a person's looks as he did those of a critter. There might be a time we had been to a "gathering" and it could have been several weeks since we had seen some of the people. On the trip home, Mama and Dad usually talked over the day. It might go like this:

Dad would say, "Mable is sure lookin' good." Mama would say, "It looks to me like she is getting fatter." Mable was plump to start with.

Or Dad might say, "It looks like Helen is fallin' away." Mama would answer, "She looked good to me."

If there was a nice, slender lady there, Dad was sure to say, "Harriet is too bony," which meant in his eyes she was far too thin to look good.

I remember a time when young, bashful brother Miles had his eye on a very pretty girl in Tryon. Miles was far too shy to ask her for a date, but he had noticed her. I overheard him describing the girl to Mama. He told her about her black, curly hair and her big blue eyes. Then he said "Gosh, Mom, she's no bigger around than a gallon bucket." He liked slender girls while Dad liked the looks of buxom women.

After being gone from the hills for a long time, I came home for a visit. I met my Aunt Elsie in the grocery store. I was a little more slender than I was when I last saw her. She stepped close to me and asked, "Billie, are you falling away?"

It took a few seconds for me to catch on to what she meant. Falling away was a bad thing to do as it might mean you were sick. It seems a person never fell away on purpose.

Out in our front yard was a hand waterpump with a short handle. The whole thing was close to the ground, just the right height for kids. When Bertie and I were barefooted, we were always supposed to stop and pump water on our feet to wash off the chickie-doo. (Instead of saying it like it was, Mama always had cute little words for the things the animals and birds left behind besides their tracks, such as, turkey doo, doggy doo and rabbit rolleys. Cow chips, of course, were either wet or dry, no problem there. When we cleaned out the barn, we always cleaned out the horse manure.)

When I was in my thirties and home visiting the folks, Dad told a funny story about a big bull-shipper. There were several people there and suddenly I felt that I was old enough to laugh with the rest of 'em, letting Dad know that I knew what the word meant that rhymed with bull-shipper. I felt much closer to Dad after that.

Chapter Twelve

Bertie and the Mouse

We had a small granary that opened out into the corral. The granary was where we kept the corn to feed the chickens and the pigs.

One day Dad rounded up Miles, Bertie and me. He took us to the granary and told us it was time to thin the mouse population. He gave us each something to whack mice with. I think we each had an old broom.

I was about six and of mouse-killing size. Bertie was four and a little young for the job. Mice were very thick and running everywhere.

Miles, Dad and I were making headway. Things were moving fast and no one saw Bertie leave. We paid no attention until she came back. Dad asked her, "Where did you go?"

Mama and Bertie coming in from the garden. Bertie was a Mama's girl.

She told him a mouse had started up her pant leg. She had reached and grabbed hold of it through her pants so it couldn't get any higher. Without saying a word, she had headed for Mama and the house. Bertie ran to Mama for everything. She hobbled all the way, leaning over holding that mouse in place.

When she reached Mama in the kitchen and told her what was wrong, Mama got the broom. She told Bertie to let the mouse loose.

Of course, the mouse ran out and Mama killed it.

Bertie came back to the granary to help finish killing mice. It never occurred to Bertie that any of us could have gotten that mouse. Bertie was a Mama's girl.

Chapter Thirteen

The Country Telephone Line

The country telephone makes quite a story. How it came to be, how the line was maintained and the fun we had listening in -- rubbering, it was called.

I don't remember talking over the phone to another kid. As I remember, Bertie and I were free to take the receiver down and rubber if we were by the phone when it rang a neighbor's ring.

When anyone was rubbering, everyone else had to be real quiet so the talkers would not know anyone, or who, was listening in. I don't remember Dad or Miles ever listening in, just Mama and the girls.

People were very careful not to talk of things everyone shouldn't know. It was nice to know what your neighbors were doing.

There were times when a party at one end of the line was talking to someone at the other end who had trouble hearing. That was because there were too many receivers down. Each receiver down weakened the line. In that case, it was a good idea for the listeners to hang up. They always did.

It could be, though, that the batteries in one of the phones was getting low. We had to watch those batteries. It was a good idea to replace them as soon as they started to weaken. One sign of weakened batteries was when your phone rang very softly or only tinkled.

Then there was butting in. If the two people talking did not know the whole story and the listener-in knew the real facts, it was proper for her to butt in and tell the rest of the story. A three-way conversation was not uncommon.

If someone needed the phone for an emergency and he or she took down the receiver and heard two people just passing the time of day, it was proper for the would-be caller to interrupt and ask for the line.

Mama used to tease Dad. She said she could tell who he was talking to by how loud he yelled over the phone. Once he was yelling at the top of his voice. Mama said, "That's Nate Trego." Nate was at the far end of the line. Dad just grinned and kept on yelling.

Each family had a different ring. I remember most of the rings on our line. To ring Central was one long ring. Central was southwest of our place about six miles, at the ranch of Mr. William Lawyer. I told in my other book, *Bertie and Me,* how kind, old Mr. Lawyer had one leg shorter than the other and walked with a decided limp. He was at our house taking care of trouble with our phone when I told little four-year-old Bertie to show him how he walked. Bertie waddled the full length of our kitchen with her little arms dangling in front of her as she limped. Mama scolded her. Mr. Lawyer just laughed.

Bill Lawyer was instumental in getting the phone lines and the phones up in the Sandhills. He made a deal with the cooperative phone company to have Central at his house and keep all the phone lines on his line in good working order for forty dollars a year.

Dad with his pipe.

Having a switchboard in your house meant that someone of the family must be within hearing distance of the phone twenty-four hours a day. Mr. and Mrs. Lawyer had ten children, perfect for having Central in their home. Any kid over six years old could operate a switchboard.

The Lawyer family had the switchboard at their house for eight years. I always envied the Lawyer kids.

Chapter Fourteen

THE 1919 SCHOOL CHRISTMAS PROGRAM AT DISTRICT 58

Bertie was five years old and I was seven. It was her first year in school and my second. Each year the teacher and pupils were expected to "put on a program." The teacher taught the kids pieces, songs and maybe a skit of some kind. It must have been pretty sad, but it was taken very seriously at the time. The program was given the last Friday night before the two-week Christmas vacation started.

It was Christmas of 1919 and the night for the Christmas program. It was very, very cold with snow on the ground. We lived twice as far from the school-house as any of the other kids. We knew the others would be there and Bertie and I were in the program and had to be there. At least we set up such a howl that Dad agreed to take us.

It was too cold to take the Ford. The radiator would have frozen up before we made it to the first gate. The only transportation we had was a team of horses hitched to the lumber wagon.

Dad put a thick layer of hay in the bottom of the wagon along with some blankets and the old buffalo robe from the old Ford. All the sideboards were on the lumber wagon, three high, thus breaking some of the wind.

Mama, Bertie and I cozied down in the hay. We were covered with all those covers. Dad hitched a tough team of horses to the wagon and we were on our way to celebrate Christmas.

It was so cold that Dad and Miles walked part of the distance on the off-wind side of the wagon as Dad drove the team. Walking was warmer than riding in the wagon seat.

We were almost to the schoolhouse when Bertie and I looked out from under the robe and spotted an iron bolt on one of the sideboards. It was covered with frost. It looked like cake frosting. Bertie gave it a lick and her tongue stuck fast.

Bertie tried to cry, but found that was pretty hard to do with her tongue stuck to the bolt. She managed to pull it loose, but it was bleeding badly.

The only thing Mama had to clean Bertie up with was snow. She used snow to stop the bleeding and to clean the blood off Bertie's dress and coat.

Bertie swears that I told her to stick her tongue on that bolt. I don't remember that I did, but I don't remember that I didn't either.

The others were all there when we arrived. Bertie, being the youngest kid in school, was to open the program with a piece she had memorized. She walked out to the open spot on the floor after the sheet (curtain) was pulled back. With a skinned tongue and wearing a bloody dress, she spoke her piece:

A little smile, a little song,
Does much to help this world along.

This is the lumber wagon that Bertie got her tongue stuck on the winter we went to the Christmas program.

After I wrote this story, Bertie read it and asked, "How about telling the time you got *your* tongue stuck to the pump handle?"

After the incident in the wagon, the folks told us we should never stick our tongues on frosted iron. They said if it ever happened again, the other one of us should get some water and pour it on the stuck tongue and it would come loose without leaving any skin behind.

One cold morning we were out in the front yard where there was an iron pump. I noticed the frost on the pump handle. I decided I would see if I could stick my tongue on the frost and get it off before it stuck. I tried and found myself stuck to the pump handle.

I couldn't talk but made noises in my throat and waved my arms until I got Bertie's attention. She knew just what to do: run into the house and get some water. Which she did.

She came out on the run carrying the teakettle.

Mama was following Bertie out to see what she was going to do with a tea-kettle of boiling water. She stopped Bertie in time and we learned that cold water would do the trick.

Here is Bertie again. She just asked me if I remembered the song we opened one of our programs with:

How do you do, everybody, how do you do.
From the Sandhills of Nebraska
This is what I want to ask ya'
How are you, everybody, how are you?

I have no idea who the composer of that song was.

Chapter Fifteen

GETTING STUCK

The road or trail from Tryon on west to Flats and Arthur went within four feet of our barn door. The road from the east came through our horse pasture. There was a large wooden gate that swung on hinges right at the corner of the corral. That nice gate let the traveler into our barnyard, but he had better stop and close it after he drove through.

He (the traveler) drove about two hundred feet and came to another gate, a barbed-wire one this time. It was longer than most gates as we had to pull the hay stacker through it when haying started. This gate also had to be closed after going through. We often had a night horse or some other animal shut in the barnyard. The gates had to be closed.

Bertie and Jack Ratzburg, her first boyfriend. They're sitting on Jack's Roadster.

Old cars, some Model T's, on the road.

After the traveler got back into his rig and took off, he was in our meadow. He traveled two or three city blocks and came to the south end of the north lake. This part of the meadow was boggy when the water was high in the spring. We tried to keep enough hay or other filling in the bad spots to make it passable.

All people that knew the road could get through without getting stuck. Let some city fella' come along and he might get stuck. When that happened, it was up to Dad or Miles to get a horse or horses to pull him out, depending on how badly he was stuck.

One day Dad and Miles were gone and I saw a car get stuck in our bog. I walked down. There were two strangers (men). I asked them if they needed help. They said they did.

I told them there was a team of horses in the barn and as soon as I got them harnessed, I'd come down and pull them out.

I hurried back to the barn. I'd never harnessed a horse by myself before. I worked hard and tried to work fast, but I guess I took a long time.

I'd just finished the job and was leading the horses out of the barn when the stuck car pulled up in front of me. The men were able to dig themselves out during the time it took me to get the team harnessed. I was thinking how big I would feel after I pulled them out.

They thanked me and gave me an orange. To me that orange looked wonderful. We didn't get an orange very often up there. I was proud of that orange, but I had to put the horses back in their stalls and unharnessed before I got to it. Then I picked it up and ran to the house to show Mama and Bertie.

I peeled my orange and divided it as nearly as I could into five equal parts. I gave Mama and Bertie each their share and I ate mine. It sure was good. Then I got on my horse and took Miles his share. He was working in the south meadow.

I knew that Dad had gone north when he left on his horse that afternoon. I rode north until I found Dad and gave him his share of the orange.

Getting the orange turned out to be better than if I had been able to pull the fellows out of the mudhole and they had given me a dollar.

Chapter Sixteen

THE OLD PRIVY

Sometimes it's fun to think of the old privy. The first picture that comes to mind is seeing it from the outside. It was a building everyone ignored. That is, until he or she needed it. Many places it was hidden or partly hidden from plain sight. One thing for sure, the shape was always the same. As soon as you spotted it, no matter where you were, you knew what it was and what it was for.

As I first recall our old privy, it sat about sixty feet northwest from our back kitchen door. It was very close to the big cowchip pile which partly camouflaged it from the barn along with some scrawny cottonwood trees and the chicken house.

In those days the men weren't supposed to see the women going to the privy. I don't know why, but it seemed we always tried to slip "out back" when no one saw you.

Mama always said the word "privy" in a hushed tone. The word was never used in mixed company. Also being near the cow chip pile, if a man saw a woman heading in that direction, they might think she was going after chips for the stove.

There were two sizes, a two-holer and a three-holer. Ours was a small, conservative two-holer, one big hole and one much smaller hole, both on the level comfort-

One of those distinctive privies.

able for adults. The kid got up there the best he or she could unless there was an adult along to boost the kid up.

The three-holer (the deluxe) was two large holes on the adult level and one smaller hole on a shorter ledge that any kid could climb on. The seat around the adult holes was always nice and shiny from so much sitting. I don't remember the kid's hole being shiny. I guess the kid didn't spend much time sitting and thinking.

There were two things one had to be on the lookout for. Wasps liked to build their nests in outhouses. I don't remember any of us being stung by wasps in the privy, but we heard of it happening.

The other scary thing was getting locked in. Nailed to the outside of the doorframe was a piece of wood about four inches long and an inch thick. The person leaving the privy was supposed to close the door and turn that knob. This was to keep the door from flapping in a wind and to keep the tumbleweeds and dirt from blowing in. The danger here was if a couple of little girls were inside with the door closed, that knob might slip over and lock them in.

This happened to Bertie and me one time and we panicked. We screamed, hollered and cried. We pounded on the door. We kept this up until Mama heard us from in the house and came to our rescue.

Mama laughed as she always did if nothing serious happened to us. That let us know it wasn't as bad as we thought. Then she showed us what to do if it ever happened again.

All we had to do was tear a few sheets from that catalog that was always handy, fold the sheets enough times to make it strong enough to reach through the crack and lift the knob.

Another thing I remember about these little buildings is that they always faced the south.

After a few years, the privy had to be moved. To do this, a hole was dug five or six feet deep. The old privy building fit the new hole. It looked the same as it did before only in a new spot. The old hole was filled in.

When the folks moved ours, they set it about sixty feet southeast of the house. It still faced the south and away from the house. We could leave the door open on

Horse and rider. Note the privy in the background.

nice days and look out over the south meadow lake. We could sit there and watch ducks or mud hens swim around. It was even a good place to hide out for a while.

Privies were very cold places in the winter. There were many cracks in the structure. The wind blew almost as hard inside little building as it did outside.

When it snowed one had to brush the snow off the seat. One dashed to the privy on cold days and dashed back to the house as fast as possible. The worst part for a girl kid was unbuttoning the drop seat of the long winter underwear. There were three or four buttons back there and, of course, they had to buttoned up again before leaving. A kid didn't fool around long when she went to the outhouse on cold, snowy days. The same was true at school. If it wasn't too cold a kid didn't put on a coat, he or she just ran very fast.

Chapter Seventeen

THE DRUNKEN DUCK HUNTERS

Many groups of duck hunters came to our ranch each fall. A narrow, slow-flowing stream connected the nice-sized lake in our north meadow to another lake in the south meadow. Our place was a popular hunting place since it didn't take a lot of walking to hunt our lakes.

There was also a small lake just over a rise north of the north meadow lake. The rise was a great place for hunters to sneak over and surprise a flock of ducks.

Ducks were very thick in those days. If the hunters were sober and could shoot straight, there would sure enough be a few ducks leaving that lake without their mates.

Duck hunting season was a time certain groups of men from the cities looked forward to. They brought enough whisky and shotgun shells to last three or four days and camped in our barnyard. We became acquainted with them and we enjoyed them being there. They livened things up. The hunters enjoyed the peace and quiet. We kids enjoyed the excitement.

"Uncle" Joe Snyder with his ducks.

One fall, two of the men brought their wives. They stayed in the house with us. The women helped Mama with the housework and the men hunted. It was a social time for all of us.

We always got up early at our house. Early morning was the prime time to hunt ducks, just as they came into the lakes for their breakfasts. Dad, Miles, Bertie and I did the morning chores. The hunters went hunting. Mama and the wives prepared breakfast.

A part of this story is very clear in my mind. The hunters (our company) were going home that day. The men had come back from their morning hunting. The chores were finished and everyone was in the kitchen.

The men were at the table eating and Mama was frying pancakes. The men weren't talking and "joshing" as usual. That meant it was a good time for a kid to keep quiet. Bertie and I were standing around trying to stay out of the circle of tension.

One of the city women went out to the privy. As I said before, by leaving the privy door open, one had a good view of the lake just south of the garden.

The City Lady came back into the house. She had a whispered conversation with Mama. Mama hurriedly handed over the pancake turner to her and quietly left the kitchen by way of the north door. What on earth had happened? Mama never quit cooking right in the middle of making breakfast.

The next thing I remember was Mama walking in the south kitchen door carrying some dead ducks. Mama was a good duck hunter, one who didn't drink whiskey. The hunters had not gotten any ducks that morning. Whether the whiskey outlasted the shotgun shells or they were too drunk to shoot straight, I don't know. Their wives had been plenty put out when the men came in that morning, drunk and without any ducks.

As the City Lady was sitting in the privy looking out over the lake, she saw a flock of ducks come down and light in the garden lake. That was what the whispered conversation was about. Mama quietly slipped out the north door and grabbed the shotgun that was kept on the north porch.

Our beloved hunting dog named Fanny went with her. She was as great at retrieving as she was at pointing out pheasants. One couldn't pick up a gun without Fanny at your heels.

Mama and Fanny slipped around to the garden south of the house without the men or the ducks seeing her. The men were all looking into their plates and eating the pancakes Mama had just cooked. The City Lady with the pancake turner kept the cakes coming to the table.

Miles hunting with his dog, Fanny

I can't help but believe Dad saw Mama leave and knew what she was up to. The grin on Dad's face as Mama walked in the south door carrying dead ducks told Bertie and me everything was all right now. Mama had shot the ducks, Fanny had retrieved them from where they fell into the lake and Mama was back in the house before any of the morning hunters knew she had left the kitchen.

Dad joshed the hunters, telling them his wife was a better hunter than they were. The atmosphere in the kitchen loosened up and the wives had the last laugh. The company left that morning.

The men came back many times, but I don't believe they ever brought their wives again.

Chapter Eighteen

FISHING

It seems a lot of our life centered around our lakes. During the fall of the year, the good-natured duck hunters livened things up for a time. During the long winter months there was skating and trapping muskrats. (The first skates I remember owning were a pair of little bob-skates that fastened on my shoes. They had two runners instead of one. Bertie had a pair just like them.)

As the weather warmed up in the spring, it was always exciting when the fish started biting. We had only bullhead fish in our lakes. The larger lakes, such as Schick Lake and the Diamond Bar Lake had game fish. That meant they had sunfish, crappy and bluegills. Those white fish with shiny scales were much prettier than bullheads. I always felt bullheads were a poor man's fish and not as classy as the game fish and wished we had game fish in our lakes. Later, when I had a chance to eat game fish and discovered they had all those little bones in their flesh, I liked our bullheads just fine.

Dad loved to fish and liked to eat them, too. He said if game fish got started in our lakes they would kill off the bullheads. For eating, Dad liked the bullheads best.

Dad seemed to know when the fish would be biting. He may have gone by this little jingle that he taught us kids:

When the wind is in the east
It's neither fit for man nor beast.

Bertie learned to fish in the Sandhills. This is a trout she caught in Yellowstone Park. She was a real fisherwoman.

When the wind is in the north,
Skilled fishermen go not forth.

When the wind is in the south,
It blows the bait in the fish's mouth.
When the wind is in the west
Then it's at its very best.

I remember many evenings Dad saying, "I think the fish might be biting." That meant we all got our bamboo fishing poles out. The two girl kids took a spade and a worm can and went out east of the barn to the manure pile and dug grub worms for bait.

Mama loved to fish and was always with us. That meant five or six people lined along the shore of the lake, each with a fish line in the water and a bright-colored bobber floating over it. We could catch fish from the bank, but fishing was better if we could get into deeper water. We didn't own a boat yet.

If we had plenty of time to get back to the house and get our fish cleaned before dark, Dad hitched a team of horses to the lumber wagon. We all crawled in and rode down to the lake. Dad backed the wagon out into the lake and we fished from the wagon. That was fun and we caught more fish. It seemed like Dad could make anything better with a team and a lumber wagon.

Whenever one of us caught a bigger fish than usual, we all got excited and settled down to more serious fishing. I remember those fishing evenings as always being fun. Dad was ever so jolly when he was fishing and that made it fun for all of us.

One time when we were fishing from the wagon, I was standing in the back, the best spot. We had been there for some time and were catching lots of fish. I was having fun. I heard Dad say, "Pull in your lines; the sun is getting low. It's time to get home and get these fish cleaned and get at the chores."

I thought I'd leave my line out there a minute longer. The first thing I knew I was in the water, headfirst. By the time I came up sputtering, the team, wagon and the rest of the family were on the bank laughing.

Dad had spoken and I hadn't moved as fast as the rest of them. Dad slapped the team on the rump with the reins, making them jump and jerk the wagon enough to dump me out headfirst. It was kind of a joke and a lesson as well. When something like that happened to a kid, the kid was supposed to laugh along with the rest. At times it was hard to do and that was one of those times.

As I've said, we had only bullheads in our lakes. A bullhead has a slick skin, no scales like a game fish.

This was the way we cleaned and dressed bullheads:

Our fish cleaning spot had a couple of sawhorses side by side. There was a hammer on each sawhorse and a large nail tapped in the wood. We had the fish in a tub of water on the ground between the sawhorses. Most of the fish were still alive, as we kept them in water since catching them.

A person (it might be a kid, it might be Mama or Dad), straddled each sawhorse. Oh yes, each straddler had a sharp knife and a pair of pliers at hand. We called pliers 'pinchers' in those days.

The fish cleaner pulled the nail out of the sawhorse. He held the nail in his left hand and reached into the tub with his right hand and grabbed a wiggly fish. He placed the fish on the sawhorse, belly down, with the fish's chin and throat flat on the board. Holding the fish down with the heel of his left hand, he centered the nail in the fish's head, picked up the hammer with his right hand and drove the nail through the fish's head and into the board far enough to hold the fish. If the fish wiggled out from under your hand and dropped in dirt, you had to wash it off and start all over.

Fishing from the bank at Snyder Lake with friends from Tryon.

As soon as the nail went through the fish's head, the fish was dead. The fish cleaner laid the hammer down, picked up the sharp knife and cut the fish across the back of the neck. He slit the skin down the back a quarter of an inch. He lay the knife down and picked up the pinchers, gripped the right side of the skin and pulled the skin off, then did the same on the left side. He put the pliers down, picked up the knife and finished cutting the head off.

There was a large pan of fresh water on the ground nearby. He tossed his skinned fish in the pan of water, usually hitting the pan on the first toss. He put the knife down and picked up the hammer. Using the claw part of the hammer, he pulled out the nail that still had the fishhead on it. He pulled the nail out of the head and threw the head into an old pail nearby.

It didn't matter if he missed that bucket. The bucket of heads, along with the fish insides, was taken down and dumped back into the lake for the live bullheads to eat and grow on so they could be caught and cleaned and their insides put back into the lake for a future bunch of fish. The fish cleaner reached into the tub of fish again and kept at it until the fish were all beheaded and skinned.

The next job was done by the girl kids, Bertie and me. We picked up the pan of skinned, beheaded fish and put it on a table. With a sharp knife, we slit each fish down the belly and scraped his insides out, saving all the fish eggs.

Many of the fish had big bellies, which meant they were full of eggs. It was exciting to have a good mess of fish eggs. We rolled them in cornmeal, fried them and ate them.

In the spring or early summer, the female fish were full of eggs. There were thousands of eggs in each one. They were in two sacks that were joined together, resembling the shape of the mountain oysters taken out of the bull calves at branding time. Getting the eggs just before the fish was ready to lay them, you had a delicious bit of fish roe.

Another thing that made cleaning fish fun was to see which one of us could find the most unpopped blubbers in her fish. The blubber is a white air sack found at the back of the fish throat.

Mama finished frying the fish we cleaned and the family sat down to a great feed. As I remember, at the fish feeds, all we ate was fish and homemade bread and homemade butter.

The flesh from a bullhead is yellow. Salmon is red and all other fish flesh is white. To me, as to many other Sandhillers, the bullhead has far the best flavor.

I remember one incident. Our good neighbor, Nate Trego, had been sick for a long time and had no appetite. Someone told Dad that Nate had said he thought he could eat bullheads.

It was early fall and the fish had quit biting in our area. Dad was determined to get Nate some bullheads and finally heard of a place quite a distance from our place. Dad and Mama took fishing gear and hurried to the spot. Sure enough, they came back with some bullheads Mr. Trego was able to enjoy.

The Snyders were not the only Sandhillers to enjoy a good fish fry. Each summer there was a big fish fry at either Diamond Bar Lake or Schick Lake. The word was well circulated and everyone who enjoyed fish or fishing came.

There were many people with their own bait and poles lined up on the lake bank fishing. This was on a Sunday, the day people and horses were resting. I have one snapshot showing two little girls in the line of fishermen holding fish poles. They are dressed in their Sunday best.

Cecilia Davis preparing fish at a fish fry.

On these days there was a big crowd, some people fishing, some people cleaning fish and others frying fish over a campfire in skillets with lard someone brought. Since there was a large crowd to feed, they needed fish in a hurry.

There was always a seine available. It was a fishnet, four-feet wide and twenty-five feet long, with a six-foot pole at each end. Two big, strong men took off their boots and socks. Each picked up one end of the spread-out seine and waded out into the lake. They made a large circle and came back to shore. Usually there were hundreds of flopping fish among quite a bit of green moss when the seiners shook the seine out real good.

Neighbors enjoying a Sunday on Schick Lake.

Fishing from a boat at Schick Lake.

Now everyone got involved, including kids who were so inclined. They got down there among the fish and moss and started throwing the keepers into buckets and the ones that were too small to keep back into the lake. I loved this part as it was exciting. I hope those fish didn't know we were being unsportsmanlike.

Soon the bank was cleared of fish and anything that needed to be back in the water to live. I remember walking around once, taking everything in. I saw my Dad's leather jacket almost on the ground. It was hanging on two sticks near where the women were busy frying fish.

Summertime in the Sandhills.

I picked up his jacket and started looking for him. When I found him, I told him I had found his jacket on the ground. He hurriedly took it and went back to where they were frying fish. He told me in a why-can't-you-mind-your-own-business voice that he had placed his jacket there to keep the flour from blowing out of the pan they were flouring the fish in.

It must have been a windy day, but I hadn't noticed that. The kind of a kid I was, it's a wonder I hadn't stepped in the flour pan while taking care of things.

I was always trying to make points with my dad, but that time I lost a few.

Chapter Nineteen

ROUNDUPS

Other get-togethers for Sandhill people were the roundups we had each summer. These are now called rodeos and are very different. We had no ready-made corrals. We had no chutes to run the broncs in so they could be easily saddled and readied for the rider. The bronc rider had to mount from the ground, the same as any other rider.

The little Sunday Roundups were held at Tryon or Flats. The big three-day roundups came into being a few years later.

This is the way we did it in the teens and early twenties. There were no trucks or trailers in those days. The stock was rounded up and herded to the location where a tempory corral had been built.

Hank Embry brought his covered wagon to participate in the roundup at the creek at the Harshfield place.

Harry Thresher, Mary Frances McCullough and Miles. Cars are lined up for the roundup in the background.

The people did not have to be rounded up. They just came from far and near. The cars with the spectators made a semi-circle around the corral.

The participants were the sons of local ranchers or ranch hands. There might be a few cowboys who drifted in from outside our area. The names of the young men I remember are: Slits Coker, the Trego boys, Bill and Mose, and the Kramer boys, George and Charley. They were bronc riders. There had to have been others but I was only a kid and do not remember them. I just talked to Marvin Platt on the phone. He was a kid at the same roundups as I and he doesn't remember any more names either. However, we always had enough riders for a good show.

Mama and the Native Americans at their tent at the Harshfield Roundup.

The judges were the old timers like my dad, Bert Snyder; our neighbor, Nate Trego; or County Judge Johnson of Tryon. Of course, there was no microphone. The announcer held a big megaphone to his mouth while riding around the arena telling the onlookers the name of the next rider and the name of the horse he would be riding.

Miles and Nellie camping out at the Tryon Roundup.

Shorty Ricker at a Hershey Roundup in 1922.
(Photo courtesy of Vernon Combs.)

*Harshfield Roundup.
Cars are parked up on
the hill looking down
in the valley at the
roundup performance.*

*Native Americans at their tent
at the Harshfield Roundup.*

The bucking horses used at these roundups were horses that any rancher might have in his string that couldn't be broken for saddle horses. They were referred to as outlaws. We had outlaw horses and outlaw men in the Sandhills. Everyone knew the outlaw horses. As yet none of us knew the outlaw young man among us.

Stan Barent being bucked off a bronco at the Hershey Roundup.
(Photo courtesy of Vernon Combs.)

I remember well the outlaw bucking horse that we owned. We had named her Maude. She could not be broken for a saddle horse. Dad tried to break her for a workhorse. That didn't work either so we started taking her to the roundups as a bucking horse. She got real good at bucking off most of her riders.

Later Dad sold her to Lou Cougar to go in his bunch of bucking stock. Lou renamed her Carry Nation. I was proud of the fact that we once owned one of Lou

Line up cowboys at the Harshfield Roundup on Birdwood Creek.

Cougar's bucking horses. I always watched for her to be the next bronc to be ridden and then told everyone within listening distance she used to belong to us.

Our outlaw handsome young man was a neighbor boy. He was at most of our roundups. He was a great showman. His name was John Hunter. John had two beautiful horses he had trained for Roman Riding. The horses would travel side by side at the same gait, thus making a Roman Team. John was a very striking sight standing with one foot on each horse as they moved around the circle in front of the cars. We all looked forward to this event. Little did we know that within a few years our John Hunter would be put in the state pen for stealing his neighbor's cattle.

Years later, when John was released from the pen, he got into big-time bootlegging. A few years later he mysteriously disappeared. Seven years after his disappearance, his bones were discovered buried in a barn south of Maxwell. John's bones are now buried in the North Platte Cemetery. You see, we really did have a real outlaw among us.

John Hunter Roman Riding on his horses.
(Photo courtesy of Vernon Combs.)

I don't know where poor old Carry Nation's bones are. Wherever they are, they earned their rest, bucking all those cowboys off for our entertainment.

There were several events at those little Sunday Roundups. The Wild Bronc Riding was the most exciting. It was done so much differently then than it is today. I will do my best to describe the way I remember it.

A good roper walked in among the circle of broncs with his rope ready to throw. He soon came out with the bronc he had gone after. If the bronc was fighting the rope around his neck, a man standing by with a twitch (a small leather loop on a stick) would wrestle the bronc until he got the leather loop on his ear, then he twisted the stick tight. This was called earring him down.

The pain the horse got from this made him motionless. As soon as the horse quieted down, a halter was slipped on him. The throw rope was removed. A blind-fold was slipped under the halter. The bronc rider stood by with his blanket and saddle which he quickly threw on the horse. He pulled the cinch together and as tight as the horse would allow. The rider then mounted the horse as fast as possible. The blindfold was pulled from the halter and the bronc either took off pitching or he balked and wouldn't move, in which case, the rider got another horse.

If the horse pitched, the rider either got thrown or rode the horse to a standstill. If the horse was ridden to a standstill the cowboy dismounted the best way he could and got away from the horse fast as possible.

In the old days, the rider had to ride his horse to a standstill to be in the money. There was no time limit as there is today. I think the excitement in all of this was that we knew the rider and the horse. To me, roundups were never as much fun after they got bigger.

There was a big three-day roundup in Hershey starting June 22, 1922. The following article is from "*The Hershey Times.*"

WHOOP-E-E—LET'ER BUCK!!
THREE BIG DAYS ROUND UP STARTS TO-DAY

Today is the first day of the Hershey Roundup. Preparations have been made for an immense crowd, attractions are in readiness, and the big show will start off with the parade through the main streets to the Rodeo grounds at 1:30 P.M. today.

The Combs Brothers inform us they have fifty of the wildest outlaw horses that can be secured, twenty head of real, twisty mules and about twenty-five head of calves already in the corrals.

Riders have been arriving nearly every day. Among them are:—Curley Griffith, of Texas; Dan Offit, of Beaver City; Dale Archer of Kansas; Tom Ricker, of Texas; Eddie Wright, of Wyoming; Chas. Swartz, of Dakota; Chas. Phillips, of Dakota; Lew Cogger and bunch of riders, of Paxton; Less Coker and bunch of riders, of Sutherland; a bunch of riders from Brady, besides a great array of home riders. There'll be something stirring every minute when this bunch gets to moving.

In addition to the riding there will be relay races, potato races, fancy trick riding by lady riders, fancy roping and various stunts usually at a Rodeo.

Saturday afternoon, "Telescope," the mule that has never been ridden, the mule that has thrown over one hundred and thirty riders, will be brought out. The bunch of riders here claim he will be ridden, while the owners of the mule claim no man can ride him. About two hundred fans from Maxwell are expected here Saturday to witness the attempts to ride Telescope. Maxwell is the home of this famous mule.

Admission to the ground is 25 and 50c.

In the evenings there will be the big platform dance, band music, and fun galore on the streets. Special motion pictures Friday and Saturday nights at the opera house.

You cannot afford to miss the big show.

The following is from a flyer put out by Thos. Stebbins and the Combs Brothers advertising North Platte's 1926 Rodeo(*Flyer courtesy of Vernon Combs*):

Price List and Rules Nebraska's Greatest Rodeo
NORTH PLATTE, NEBR. RODEO
JULY 1-2-3, 1926
Under Auspices of
NORTH PLATTE VOLUNTEER FIRE DEPT.
THE MONEY IS HERE, COWBOY COME
AND GET IT!
Thos. STEBBINS, North Platte, Nebr. Promoter.
COMBS BROTHERS, Hershey Nebr. Managers.
BRING YOUR OWN SADDLES

SPECIAL NOTICE

The management reserves the right to refuse the entry of any contestant violating the general rules, dishonesty in the competitions or who has proved to be an undesirable character at any recognized cowboy contest.

GENERAL RULES

Every contestant must have his or her complete outfit, saddle, bridle and blanket, and no cowboy will be entered unless he is willing to wear his big hat and boots at all times. If you are ashamed of being a cowboy, don't come.

The management assumes no responsibility for accidents, or injury to contestants or stock, and each participant by the act of entry or participation waives all claim against the management for any injuries they or their stock may sustain.

The management reserves the right to withdraw any contestant's name and entry for any of the following reasons, to-wit:

BEING UNDER THE INFLUENCE OF INTOXICANTS.

ROWDYISM.

QUARRELING WITH JUDGES OR OFFICIALS.

ABUSING STOCK.

FAILING TO GIVE ASSISTANCE WHEN REQUESTED TO DO SO BY ARENA DIRECTOR.

NOT BEING READY FOR EVENTS IN WHICH THEY ARE CALLED.

At this contest the management proposes to run a fast, snappy program, better than any contest ever held in this part of the state and every contestant is required to lend his assistance in the matter of keeping the program moving and up to top notch all the time.

ANY CONTESTANT WITHDRAWING FROM ANY EVENT *in which he is entered or refusing to ride, rope or display his skill when called upon, will be disqualified in all events in which he is entered.*

Any event must receive at least one more entry than there are purses in that event, in order to constitute a contest.

Should there be so many entries in any event that the management should deem it inadvisable to allow all of them to compete in one day, then the management reserves the right to split them up over two days.

Identification numbers will be issued to every contestant. These MUST *be worn in a visible manner at all times while on the field.* EVERY *contestant* MUST HAVE A SADDLE *and ride in each and every grand entry and parade. Any contestant failing to do so or failing to properly display their identification numbers will be disqualified.*

THERE WILL BE ABSOLUTELY NO SUBSTITUTING AT THIS CONTEST.

THESE *rules may be changed or added to if the judges consider conditions necessary, and their decision is final.*

More cowboys - Can you recognize any men or horses?

CHAMPIONSHIP BRONK RIDING CONTEST

Purse, $600.00

Entrance Fee, $7.50

Three Days, Day money-1ˢᵗ, $50.00; 2ⁿᵈ, $30.00; 3ʳᵈ, $20.00.

Finals—1ˢᵗ, $150.00; 2ⁿᵈ, $100.00; 3ʳᵈ, $50.00.

This is a four horse average contest.

CONDITIONS—*Riders to draw for mounts and ride as often as the judges require.*

Each rider shall be required to cinch his own saddle and no two men will be allowed to pull the cinch on a horse. If a saddle is not cinched tight enough and comes off, rider will be given a re-ride, but rider will be disqualified for cheating horse in any manner when it is plain to judges that rider has purposely cheated horse to keep the horse from doing its best.

All spur rowels must be covered and no steel showing. Riding to be done with plain halter and one rein, no knots or wraps around the hand, no tape allowed on rein or stirrups. Pulling horse's head will be counted against the rider. Rein to come up same side of horse's neck as hand you ride with. Rider must hold reins at least six inches above horse's neck. Horses to be saddled in chute on the field. Rider must leave starting place with both feet in the stirrups and both spurs against the shoulders, must scratch front first five jumps, then scratch high behind. Rider must ride with one hand free and not change hands on rein. Chaps, spurs, saddle and boots to be passed on by judges. Riders to ride last two mounts without chaps.

Any of the following offenses disqualifies the rider:

Being bucked off.

Changing hands on the reins.

Wrapping rein around hand.

Losing stirrup.

Pulling leather.

Failing to leave starting place with spur against the shoulder.

Not being ready when called on to ride.

CHAMPIONSHIP STEER WRESTLING CONTEST

Purse, $600.00

Entrance Fee, $7.50

Three Days, Day Money—1st, $50.00; 2nd, $30.00; 3rd, $20.00.

Total on Three Steers—1st, $150.00; 2nd, $100.00; 3rd, $50.00.

CONDITIONS—*Steers will be numbered and drawn for, and any wrestler guilty of tampering with steers, chute or numbers will be disqualified.*

Wrestler and hazer will be allowed to leave the chute with steer, and wrestler's mount and steer may be Lap-and-Tap when crossing dead line, but wrestler must not have hand on steer or leap before crossing dead line, penalty not less than 15 seconds.

Steer belongs to wrestler when he crosses dead line. All steers must be thrown by hand. This is a twist-down contest. Wrestler must stop steer and twist him down. If steer is accidentally knocked down, he must be let up on all four feet and thrown again, and should steer start running after once being stopped and then be thrown by wrestler putting horns against the ground, then steer must be let up again and twisted down.

Wrestler to throw steer, and signal judges with one hand for time. Steer will be considered down when he is lying flat on his side, all feet out and head straight. Should wrestler let steer up before being told to do so by field judge, 30 seconds will be added to his time.

Should wrestler loosen or knock off horn he shall receive no time on steer. Wrestler must be ready and take steer in his turn, or ten seconds will be added to his time. Best total time on all steers wins final money.

A time limit of two minutes will be placed on wrestling and if a wrestler has caught his steer but has not been able to throw him when the two minutes have expired he will be signaled to retire from the field and given no time.

CHAMPIONSHIP CALF ROPING CONTEST

Purse, $600.00

Entrance Fee, $15.00

50 percent of entrance fee to be added to finals.

Three Days' Day Money—1ˢᵗ, $50.00; 2ⁿᵈ, $30.00; 3ʳᵈ, $20.00.

Total on Three Calves—1ˢᵗ, $150.00; 2ⁿᵈ, $100.00; 3ʳᵈ, $50.00.

CONDITIONS—*There shall be three timekeepers, a tie judge, a foul line judge and one starter. All calves to be penned and any objectionable calf cut out.*

Calves will be given deadline start in accordance with field conditions, and when calf crosses deadline he is roper's calf regardless of what happens. Ten seconds' fine for roper's mount being over foul line when starter's flag drops.

Roper must not "bust" calf, but must go down rope and flank calf by hand, cross any three feet and tie in the proper manner.

A catch must be made with the rope that will hold calf until the roper gets to him. Tie to be passed upon by the judge, and roper will not be allowed to touch calf in any manner after signaling for time, until judgement of the tie has been pronounced by the tie judge. Calf will be left tied down as long as deemed necessary by judge to ascertain if tie is complete.

This is a catch-as-catch-can contest, but roper must adjust rope and reins in a manner to prevent his horse busting calf. Any roper busting his calf will be fined not less than ten seconds and not more than one minute, according to the willfulness of the act and the time gained thereby. Willful violation or disregard of this rule disqualifies roper.

However, if roper catches calf and stops his horse and calf runs on and busts himself, then the roper shall not be fined.

Roper shall be allowed two loops and should he miss with both loops he shall then retire from the field. Roper roping calf without turning loose the loop will be considered no catch.

CHAMPIONSHIP STEER RIDING CONTEST

Purse, $135.00
Daily—3 days—1ˢᵗ, $20.00; 2ⁿᵈ, $15.00; 3ʳᵈ, $10.00.
Riding to be done with loose rope and one hand.

————

ROMAN RACE—EACH DAY

50-30-20—Day Money
No Horses Barred

————

COWBOY PONY RACE—ONE-FOURTH MILE

Purse, $135.00
Daily—3 Days—1ˢᵗ, $20.00; 2ⁿᵈ, $15.00; 3ʳᵈ, $10.00.
Only horses used in roping and steer wrestling allowed in this race.

————

COWBOY RELAY RACE

Purse, $300.00
Daily—3 Days—1ˢᵗ, $50.00; 2ⁿᵈ, $30.00; 3ʳᵈ, $20.00.
No Horses Barred

CONDITIONS—*Each rider shall have three horses in charge of not more than two assistants. Each horse to run quarter-mile daily, changing horses each quarter-mile. Race to start with riders mounted, all horses to be saddled, riders to change horses but do not change saddles. Ten seconds fine for running through another change station, except if rider is thrown, helpers may leave station to assist in catching horse. If rider is injured, substitute may ride, using same saddle with permission of judges. No less than four strings to start in each race or this event will be cancelled. Horses having been used in one string cannot be used in another. This race is open to the world, no breed of horses barred, and no guaranteed strings entered; but this is a* COWBOY RACE *and all riders and helpers must wear a Cowboy hat. No chaps will be allowed.*

Plenty of good barns for your stock at the Fair Grounds and you will be treated royally by the citizens of North Platte.

This is a real Cowboy Contest, not a barnyard event; is governed by good rules, under good square management and every prize winner in every contest will be judged fairly and squarely and every contestant must work for his money. Let's everyone make this a real contest. Bring your outfit, Cowboy, and come on, the money's yours if you win it.

All entrance fees must be in the hands of the director by June 30 at 9 p.m. Use certified check, money order or cash payable to Thos. Stebbins, director.

Cowboys being served dinner at a roundup.

Chapter Twenty

PICKING POTATO BUGS

Our potato patch was in the meadow on the west bank of the little crick that carried the water from the lake in the north meadow to the lake in the south meadow. It wasn't a very wide crick. If a little kid got back and took a big enough run, she could jump it without getting her feet wet. The crick and the potato patch could be seen from the west window of our living room.

The patch was large enough to furnish a family of six hearty eaters with potatoes for a year with enough left over for seed potatoes to plant the crop for the following year. The kids were taught young to cut seed potatoes. We made sure to have at least one eye in each chunk of potato sliced off, leaving enough potato on the eye to produce a good sprout to come through the surface and start the plant.

Dad, Bertie and I planted potatoes. Dad hitched one horse to the plow. Bertie and I each got a bucket of cut potatoes we had readied the day before. We went to the potato patch.

Dad set the plow into the ground, starting the first furrow. Either Bertie or I stepped in behind him and placed a potato hunk (making sure the potato eye was looking to the sky) on the first end of the furrow. We stepped on it to make sure it stayed in place. We took a long, kid step and placed another piece of potato on the ground, then another step and another piece, another step and another piece.

As Dad got down the row a ways with the plow, the other kid stepped in and planted her potatoes in the same manner. We kids had to hurry to keep up with

Dad and the horse, but it always seemed to work. We did this in the forenoon and were done by dinnertime.

We tried to plant potatoes on Good Friday, as that was when everyone was supposed to plant their potatoes. Good Friday had to come late enough in March for the frost to be out of the ground. Otherwise, we had to wait for warmer weather.

The potato patch was not fenced off as no livestock ever ran loose in the meadow. With nothing to hinder their growth, the potato plants soon came through the surface. Just as they were about to blossom out, the potato bugs hit them.

This ugly bug was the size of a large pea. He had a yellow-and-brown-striped hard shell. Those bugs quickly ate the leaves off the potato plants. Mama and Dad watched the plants closely. As the potato bugs appeared, another kid job was at hand.

We took an old tin can, put a couple of inches of kerosene in the bottom and pumped a few inches of water into the can. The kerosene stayed on top of the water and killed the bugs as we dropped them in.

Bertie had her potato bug can and I had mine. We had to inspect each plant, pick off all the bugs and drop them into the kerosene. The tricky part was the eggs they laid. They were always on the underside of a leaf. They looked like a flat glob of little yellow beads. All the leaves with eggs on them had to be picked off and dropped in the bug can. It was a dirty job and we hated it. Each bug we picked up let go with a dirty drop of liquid that looked like tobacco juice. It made our hands dirty. To this day, potato bugs are my least favorite bugs.

*Mabel Gustson, Bertie and Billie
at the irrigation ditch.*

Most of the time, Bertie and I worked the potato bug picking together. She would start at one side of the patch and I'd start at the other. We'd meet in the middle. Once in a while, one of us did it alone. There is one time I'll never forget.

Mama sent me out to pick potato bugs. I got my bug can, waded the crick and was picking. I was working at the far end of a row. The meadow grass was tall around the potato patch. A snake jumped out at me.

I was, and still am, scared to death of snakes. I threw my can of potato bugs to the ground and ran to the house as fast as I could. I still remember dashing in to tell Mama that a snake jumped at me.

Mama actually liked snakes. She had no patience with anyone who was afraid of them, especially one of her kids. The only snakes we had in the meadow were the green-and-yellow-striped harmless garter snakes, but they would strike if threatened.

A short time before this, I had been playing on the idle hay stacker. There was a piece of rope hanging down from a top crosspiece. For some reason, it looked very tempting. I had grabbed the rope and backed up as far as I could. I lifted my feet off the floor to get as big a swing as possible. The only problem was the rope was too long and my butt picked up part of the floorboard, leaving quite a chunk of it in me.

Of course, I ran to Mama. She got a big needle and had me lay across her lap. She pulled my bloomers down and started digging for the sticker. She dug quite a hole and I couldn't even holler, as I shouldn't have been doing what I was doing.

She finally gave up. She said it was in too deep and she would just have to leave it there. She said in time it would dissolve, but it would be sore for a while.

Mama was disgusted with me for throwing my can of potato bugs back in the patch. She was also upset with me for running from a harmless garter snake but Mama didn't want to spank me on that sore sticker spot.

She looked at me for a minute and then said, "You've gotten yourself all heated up from running. That sticker in your 'hinny' (Mama never said butt or bottom, anything down back there was our 'hinny') might flare up, so lay across my lap again and I'll try to dig it out."

She had me go get the big needle this time. As I look back, she didn't get the sticker and I didn't get a spanking.

I don't remember who picked the rest of the bugs. It wasn't me.

Soon after the potatoes blossomed, little potatoes appeared at the end of the roots. When the little potatoes got the size of pigeon eggs, they were ready to be boiled and creamed. If this happened at the same time the peas were ready to eat, we feasted on creamed new potatoes and peas fresh from the garden.

As the potatoes grew and were ready for harvest, it was time to pick them. This was a job for the whole family. Mama and the kids went to the potato patch, each with a bucket. We pulled up the plants, picking off the potatoes that clung to the vine. We put the potatoes in the bucket and threw the vine away.

Soon Dad came out to the patch with a team of horses hitched to a harrow. He raked the soft ground with the harrow bringing the rest of the potatoes to the surface. These we picked up, making sure we got every potato. We emptied our buckets into a wagon that was standing nearby.

After the potatoes were all picked, the wagon was driven down to the dugout where all of our underground vegetables were stored.

There was still one potato job left for the kids. That was sprouting the un-eaten potatoes the next spring. When the potatoes the kid brought up from the dugout for Mama to cook started showing signs of sprouting, it was time to send a couple of little girls down there to sprout 'em. We rubbed our hands over each potato, making sure we got all the sprouts that had started to grow out of the potato eyes.

After all this work, the folks were careful to see that nothing was wasted. Bertie says she remembers one time she was peeling potatoes. She said she knows she was small since she had the pan of potatoes she was peeling sitting on the oven door. (The oven door was the workbench for a kid too short to reach the cabinet top.) Dad walked through the kitchen, looked at the potato peelings in her pan and scolded her for wasting potatoes by making the peelings too thick. He made her peel all her potato peelings over.

Today Bertie is the thinnest potato peeler I know.

Chapter Twenty-one

Before Baled Hay

Hauling hay to the cattle during the winter was another big ranch job. This was a man's job. The kids, young gals, and even men from town thought this was a fun thing. On a nice winter morning with the sun shining and no wind blowing, we liked to take a pitchfork and go out to feed cattle with Miles and Dad. As the pictures show, we were not much help.

Seven days a week during winter months, our herd of cattle had to be fed the hay we had stacked the past summer. On school days, as soon as we had finished our breakfast of beefsteak, biscuits and gravy or oatmeal and pancakes, Dad and Miles saddled the school horses for Bertie and me. During the short days of winter, the sun wouldn't be up yet, but just about. As soon as Dad and Miles turned us out the east gate headed for school, they were ready to go feed.

Miles is driving the team pulling half of the haystack over onto the sled.

Miles and his friend. Half of the haystack has been pulled onto the sled.

They harnessed and hitched up the four-horse team that was kept overnight with the school horses in the barn along with plenty of feed. The team was hooked up to a gadget made to hitch a four-horse team on. The gadget was hooked to the big sled used to haul hay out to the feed ground. They headed out to a haystack down in the meadow. Each stack would make two sleds full of hay.

They lined the sled up alongside the haystack. The gadget was unhooked from the sled and fastened to the far end of a sixty-feet-long, half-inch cable at the front left corner of the sled. Then they drove the team around the stack.

They placed the cable halfway up the stack and used a pitchfork to hold it in place as they drove the team far enough to pull the top half of the stack over onto the sled. The team had to be stopped at an exact spot or the half stack would be pulled across the sled and onto the ground.

The gadget was unfastened from the cable. They drove it to the front of the sled and fastened it back to the sled. The hay was now ready to be hauled a quarter to three-quarters of a mile to the feed ground and fed to the cattle.

As the sled of hay entered the pasture, the cattle all headed for their feed. It was a pretty sight, one I never tired of seeing, those pretty, white-faced Hereford cattle strung out after the sled. I liked it best in the spring when there were many little white-faced calves following their mamas. I still can't help but smile at any white-faced Hereford calf when I see one, even if he is half mile away.

As they reached the feed ground, Dad and Miles, or whoever was aboard, started pitching hay off the sides of the sled. It was best to have a gentle team so they could secure the reins and the horses would stop and start with the "giddups" and "whoas" as needed for leaving a row of hay along each side of the sled.

As I said, this was fun when the weather was nice. On cold, windy days, when it was snowing and the temperature was below zero, it was not fun.

This may sound like lots of work. Not so! This was the modern method for feeding cattle. The old way to feed cattle (I remember that, too) was to hitch a two-horse team to an old hayrack and pull up alongside one of the stacks and secure the team. The cattle feeder climbed up on the haystack with his pitchfork. He pitched the hay from the stack into the hayrack until he had a good, big load.

He hauled that load out to the feed ground, pitched it out to the cattle and went back for another load. This was kept up until the entire herd of cattle was fed for that day. It was done seven days a week throughout the winter or until the grass was growing in the spring.

When I was fourteen, I pestered Dad to let me learn to drive the four-horse sled team. He did, but it was not the thrill it was when I drove the two-horse stacker team at six years old.

The spring I was fifteen, I was not yet thought of as a young lady, just a big kid. As they say in the old western novels, spring came late that year. That meant there was snow on the ground in late April. The ranchers were still feeding the cattle hay.

White-faced cows and calves waiting for their breakfast.

This is how cattle were fed before we had hay sleds. (Photo courtesy of Vernon Combs.)

Maude and Marion Huffman, a young-married couple, ranched fifteen miles north of us. Maude had given birth to their third child and was just home from the hospital. She had her hands full. Mama asked me if I would like to go up and help Maude for a while. That sounded great to me as I thought a lot of Maude and it would be fun to be around a tiny baby

The folks took me up to Huffmans. The first three or four days, I helped Maude clean, cook and take care of the little kids. Then Marion found out I could drive a four-horse team on a sled. (I must have told him.) He had no help feeding his cattle, so from then on, as long as I was up at Huffmans, I helped Marion feed cattle every morning. Maude went on taking care of the kids and the house as before.

Chapter Twenty-two

THE WAY WE DRESSED

For women and girl-kids, getting dressed was no small job in the early 1900s, especially during the winter weather. First and worst was the long-legged underwear which we crawled into. This was a one-piece affair with long legs and long sleeves. It had to be buttoned all the way up the front. It also had a drop seat with at least three buttons. This drop seat had to be unbuttoned and buttoned up again every time the kid went to the privy. It was many years before zippers or velcro.

We had to have something to hold up those long, coarse, black stockings so we put on a supporter waist. This was a vest-looking affair with two supporters in front and two in the back.

The next step was to sit on the floor and put a stocking on one foot, trying to make a neat fold over the leg of underwear and pulling the stocking up over the knee. We did the same with the second leg. We stood up to fasten each stocking to the supporters, trying to keep the stocking from wrinkling.

Nellie dressed up: high-top shoes, black-ribbed stockings and even a Sunday hat.

We pulled on a pair of black sateen bloomers (homemade), a flannel petticoat and, finally, our dresses. Our dresses always had a Peter Pan collar and buttoned up the back. Mama made all of our dresses. In fact, she made everything we wore except our long underwear and our black-ribbed stockings. And she darned our stockings, especially on the knees.

Now, we were all dressed but our shoes, so we sat down on the floor again with our shoes and buttonhook. We wore black high-top button shoes that Dad half-soled when they needed it.

Billie in a homemade dress.

We had to be careful buttoning those shoes. If we happened to skip a button, we had an extra buttonhole at the top. Then we had to unbutton back down to the missed button and do it over.

If Dad built a fire in the living room early in the morning, we dressed in the corner behind that stove. That was heavenly, but it didn't happen very often. We usually dressed in the kitchen by the range while Mama was getting breakfast. If Mama wasn't baking biscuits for breakfast, we could have the oven door open. That was cozy.

The dresses we wore were nicely starched and ironed. By the time we got to school, those starched dresses were badly wrinkled. We looked fine in front but our black sateen bloomers and gray flannel

Our cousin, Sylvia Snyder, cooling her feet. Look at all the clothes she had to lift up to get them out of the water.

Billie in knickers Mama made.

petticoats showed in the back. It couldn't be helped. Girls were supposed to wear dresses and the only way we had to get to school was horseback. Sitting in the saddle wrinkled our dresses.

There came a time when I saw a picture of a girl wearing knickers in a Monkey Wards Catalog. I took the picture to Mama and asked her if she could make me a pair of them. Mama was a wonderful seamstress. We could show her a picture of something we wanted and she would get an old newspaper and cut a pattern that fit. She'd get the material and we'd soon have something that looked exactly like the picture. (What she sewed always fit me at the time, but I outgrew it as fast as I could. I wanted to get taller.)

Mama got the kind of material she needed for the knickers the next time she went to town. She made Bertie and me each a pair. We loved wearing those knickers and wore them to school. We were rid of our wrinkled dresstails.

It wasn't too long before Mama made a pair of ladies britches for herself. It took a while before Mama got up the nerve to wear them in public.

The day came when Mama, Bertie and I were out horseback riding and stopped to visit our neighbor, Mae Trego. I think it was the first time Mama had worn her knickers away from the ranch. When we went in, no one was there but Mrs. Trego, but soon a couple of the Trego men came in.

It was a very hot day and we were thirsty. Mama was sitting in a rocking chair. Bertie and I went into the kitchen to get a drink of

Billie in more knickers Mama made.

Sandhill transportation.

water. When we came back into the living room, Mama asked me to bring her a drink of water. I was puzzled. Mama always got her own drink of water before. But I went back into the kitchen and brought her a drink.

After we left Tregos, Mama told us she hadn't wanted Bill and Mose to see her walk in her knickers.

I hate to think what Mama went through to dress. She had all the things to put on we did except she wore a corset instead of a garter-belt. That thing had to be laced up and pulled tight.

I took care of Mama from the time she was ninety-five until she was one-hundred. Each morning when I dressed her, I had to put that corset on her. By that time they had come up with zippers so it wasn't so bad. I still think of cinching up a saddle on a horse when I think of Mama lacing her corset so tight.

I'll never forget the time Mama said to me, "Billie, the next time we go to North Platte, we'll have to see about getting you a corset." I screwed up all my courage. I told her she would never get me in one of those things. She never did!

What a wonderful feeling in late spring when we could shed our long underwear. It was greater yet when Mama let us go barefooted. We didn't have to put on those awful stockings. We didn't have to put on that supporter waist. We didn't have to put on the shoes and button them up. Then all Bertie and I had to bug Mama about was, " When can we go swimming?" Swimming meant putting on old clothes (a pair of old overalls and an old shirt) and going wading waist deep in the lake by the garden.

Mama in a not so ladylike pose.

When we asked Mama if we could go swimming and it was too early, her answer was always, "Gracious, NO. You'll catch your death of cold." That meant, not a chance.

Billie in sateen bloomers Mama made.

Mama made Bertie and me overalls out of dress material. These we wore at home until someone came visiting, then Mama made us go put on a dress.

Bertie and I each had one good dress for winter and one good dress for summer. Getting dressed up meant putting on our good dress and new shoes. We always called our shoes new until we started wearing them for everyday. That would be when our everyday shoes wore out. When we tried on new shoes, Mama always felt of the toes to make sure there was room for our feet to grow.

Another thing Mama made was our bloomers. She made them out of black sateen. I've read where some Mamas made their girls bloomers out of flour sacks. I don't remember any flour sack bloomers. I think Mama liked her pretty tea towels.

I remember trying on a bought coat. I don't know how come Mama bought me a coat as I was too young to care. The only thing I remember about the coat is Mama trying it on me.

We were standing by the kitchen table. There was a dish of watermelon preserves on the table within my reach. While Mama was admiring the coat, I leaned over and, with my fingers, picked a nice, big piece of preserves out of the dish and popped it into my mouth. Mama scolded me, saying I shouldn't do that. I might drop some juice on my new coat.

Bertie says she does not remember me ever having an un-homemade coat so Mama must have returned it to Monkey Wards. I don't ever remember wearing it, but I remember how good the preserve tasted.

Bertie remembers her first store-bought coat. We were looking at old pictures recently and I pointed out a snapshot of her in a very nice looking winter coat with a fur collar. Bertie was looking very proud and grown-up although she was only fourteen-years old at the time. The picture was taken while our family was living in Oregon where Bertie and I went to high school.

Bertie said, "You know, Bill, that was the first coat I had that Mama didn't make for me. I picked cherries and saved my check to buy it."

Cherry-picking time in Oregon is in the spring. That was when Bertie got her check. Since she wasn't buying her coat until fall, she put her check away to keep until the winter clothes came in the fall. Late in the summer the farmer who issued Bertie's check came out to our place and asked her to please cash it. He said he wanted to close his books for that year. Bertie cashed it, but held on to her money until she could buy her first store-bought coat.

This story goes back to the spring of 1923, when Nellie graduated from Maxwell High School. Our whole family went down to Maxwell to watch her graduate and attend the senior class play. Nellie was in the play.

Maxwell High School colors were, and still are, orange and black. After the play was over, they announced they wanted to sell all the material they had used in the play. There were many yards of black and many yards of orange. They asked people to please come back stage and look at it. They were selling it very cheap.

Mama went to look. She couldn't resist such a bargain. She bought it all.

As soon as we got home, Mama went right to work. She made up her own pattern. She cut one pattern to fit Bertie and made Bertie's dress. She cut a bigger pattern to fit me and made my dress just like Bertie's. She still had lots of material left. She cut an even bigger pattern to fit herself and made herself a dress exactly like Bertie's and mine.

The dresses had a black bottom and an orange top. Where the black was sewed on to the orange, it was done in big waves. It was springtime so we had short sleeves, but the short sleeves had some fancy black stuff sewed on the hem. The same black fancy stuff was also around the neck.

After Mama got the dresses all finished, we had to put them on and have our picture taken. There we stood, Mama with Bertie on one side and me on the other. I hated those dresses, also the picture.

I was going to put the picture in with this story but couldn't find it. After going through all the snapshots, I remembered I threw it out so I wouldn't have to look at it anymore. I called Bertie to see if she had one but she didn't. Then we got to discussing those dresses and Bertie told me she hated them, too. We had never told each other while we were kids that we hated those orange and black monstrosities.

Nellie's Maxwell High School graduation picture, 1923.

Those colors looked great on the football team uniforms, but not on mother-and-daughters' dresses.

Billie and Bertie in front of house in their first flapper outfits.

Billie and Maude McMullen in their best dresses.

Chapter Twenty-three

A Dead Person

The first dead person I ever saw was a young girl probably about eighteen-years old. She was the girl who taught our School District 58. I don't ever remember seeing her alive, so it had to have been before I started to school. I would have been four or five years old.

The teacher boarded with the family who lived two miles north of the school. Their oldest daughter, Dorothy, was just starting to school.

We heard the teacher was sick and was throwing up and hurt real bad in her stomach. I don't remember if they were able to get a doctor out to see her or not.

The next thing we heard was that the teacher was dead. Mama knew she should go over to as soon as possible to see if she could help. I sure wanted to go with her.

The next picture I have in my mind is opening the door to the cold bedroom where the teacher's body lay on a cot. The only thing I remember of what I saw was the pennies that lay on her eyelids. Mama told me that the pennies had been put there to hold her eyes closed.

As we left the room with Mama holding my hand, I wondered if they would take the pennies off her eyes before they put her in the ground. I was afraid to ask. I still don't know.

Chapter Twenty-four

THE CHICKENS

There was a lot of work to keeping chickens. The eggs had to be gathered each evening, but feeding them was the most work. During the winter and spring we fed them shelled corn, corn which had to be shelled off the cob by hand. We learned how to do that at an early age.

The only corn we raised was our sweet corn for the table. The corn for the chickens and the animals we bought by the wagonload, hauled it home and made a corn pile out by the chicken house.

I remember several of us sitting around a basket, shelling corn into it. Dad showed Bertie and me how to do it. He told us to pick up an ear of corn and push

Bertie and her pet chicken, Pete, in front of the chicken house.

Bertie and Me and Miles Too

the first row of kernels off the cob with our thumbs, then use the heels of our hands to rub the kernels off a few at a time. Year after year as we grew and our hands grew and became stronger we got good at shelling corn. And did our hands grow. Today we each have the biggest, ugliest hands I've seen on any old lady.

Each spring the old hens seemed to know when it was time for them to start setting on eggs to raise little chickens. When a hen started to act like she wanted to start settin', Mama said she was getting broody. Since her eggs had been taken out of the nest each day she did not have a nest full of eggs to set on.

When Mama found an old hen sitting on an empty nest longer than just long enough to lay an egg, she knew it was time to put that old hen in a nest where she wouldn't be bothered and to put a full setting (a dozen or more) of eggs under her. For the next three weeks, the old hen was in charge. She only came off the nest long enough to get a drink of water and eat her supper.

As far as I know the only other job the old hen had besides keeping her eggs warm was to turn each egg over every day. A setting hen has a special cluck. It's a cooing cluck. I guess you would call it chicken baby talk. Anyway, I liked to hear it.

The fun part was when the eggs started to hatch and the wet little balls pecked their way out of the eggshells. It wasn't long until those wet little chicks were fluffy yellow fellows.

The first hatched chicks try to crawl out from under the hen, but she keeps pushing them back under until all the eggs are hatched. When the chicks are hatched and dried off, the mother hen takes her babies out for a walk. She does her chicken baby talk and all the little chickens stay very close to her.

Now the kids get busy again as the shelled corn has to be ground up fine for the little chickens to eat. A corn grinder was fastened on a shed wall, just the right height to be operated by Bertie and me. It had a hopper on top just behind the wheel that we were supposed to turn. We set a bucket under the hopper to catch the ground corn.

One of us took the ground corn out to where the old hen was with her babies. We scattered the corn right in front the hen and her flock. We liked to watch those little fluffy balls peck up the corn.

Some of Bertie's chickens with their chicks.

As I've said before, we never wasted anything at our house, even broken dishes. We did not have many broken dishes. Only our good dishes were breakable. The ones we used for everyday were enamel. The enamel might chip off in places, but they wouldn't break. If we did happen to break a dish, every piece of it was saved. They were pounded into tiny pieces and fed to the chickens. It went into their craws and helped them digest their food.

We had a special place to pound the broken dishes into grit. There was a piece of two-foot long railroad rail on the ground on the south side of the chicken house. Either Bertie or I would get a hammer and the broken dish pieces.

We went out and sat on the ground by the iron and pounded the pieces to grit, letting it fall on the ground by the iron. When the chickens needed grit for their craw they knew where to go. We both liked that job and neither of us remembers a smashed thumb or finger.

When grasshopper season came on, the chickens really had a treat. We liked to watch a chicken grab a grasshopper in her beak and gobble it down real fast. The chickens helped keep the grasshopper population down.

This I don't remember, but Bertie says we had to take turns shutting the chicken house door each night. This was so nothing would get in the chicken house and disturb the sleeping chickens, most likely a coyote or a skunk. If we had forgotten to shut up the chickens until after dark, we both had to go out, as we were both "afraid of the dark."

Chapter Twenty-five

IKE AND THE WHISKEY

We had a neighbor living about three miles from our place. We all liked old Ike. Ike liked his whiskey, and he came to our place often and stopped to visit. Ike was always a gentleman, no matter how much he had been tipping the bottle. He also tried to keep from us the fact that he had been drinking.

One evening Ike rode up to our place just as Miles, Bertie and I were finishing the milking. He left his horse at the gate and came around the corner of the barn. It was early spring and we were still milking the cows in the shed. Bertie and I had finished our milking and were waiting around for Miles to finish his cow.

Ike walked up to the shed door and was talking to Miles. We could tell he had been drinking. Bertie and I were behind Ike and could see a bottle sticking out of his pocket. He was desperately trying to put his gloves in his pocket to cover up the bottle. He finally gave up on the gloves but still stood there. Bertie sneaked up behind Ike and slipped the bottle of whiskey out of his pocket. After running off with Ike's whiskey, we didn't know what to do with it. We decided it would be funny to get the pigs drunk so we poured the whiskey in the pig trough and threw the empty bottle under the bunkhouse. The pigs didn't get drunk.

I think this is the first time this story has ever been told.

While writing this story it comes to mind that I never remember a drunken cowboy on horseback ever having a wreck or hurting anyone. His beloved horse would always take him to the right gates so the fellow always got home.

Chapter Twenty-six

DAD AND THE LAME HORSE

I was always at Dad's heels while he was working around the barn, that is, if he didn't tell me to "go away."

There was a time Dad had a lame horse. I don't remember what the horse's name was. I watched Dad reach in his pocket and pull out a dime. He had his jackknife in his other hand and he cut a tiny slit in the horse's hide on his shoulder. He slipped the dime under the horse's skin.

I asked him, "Why did you do that?"

He said it might make the horse get well.

The horse did get well and lived for many years, but there came a time when Dad told me that horse had died. I asked Dad if he remembered to get his dime out of the horse's shoulder. He just laughed and said no.

I never did understand that, as Dad had always been careful with his money.

Chapter Twenty-seven

Climbing on the Cow Shed

I loved climbing around on the barn. The east side of the barn connected to the corral. The east slope of the roof was not as steep as the west side. It was easy to climb up on top of the barn.

One day I just knew I could carefully ease myself down the north rim of the roof and get over on the cowshed. The cowshed roof was a little lower and three feet away from the barn roof.

I did get one foot over on the cowshed, but I still had one foot on the barn roof and couldn't go either way. I looked down at the ground. I was thinking,

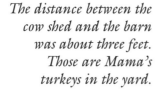

The distance between the cow shed and the barn was about three feet. Those are Mama's turkeys in the yard.

"This is farther than I've ever jumped before," but I knew I would have to jump. I was scared.

While I was trying to get up enough nerve to jump, I heard a loud, scolding voice say, "BILL, GET DOWN FROM THERE."

I was so used to doing what Dad told me to, with no effort I got the foot from the barn on the shed with the other foot.

Neither of us mentioned it to the other. I figured Dad must have been watching me from the house.

Chapter Twenty-eight

OUR BROTHER MILES

Our brother Miles was always there for any of us who needed anything. When Miles finished the eighth grade at our little seven-month country school, he wanted to go on to high school. Dad said he needed Miles on the ranch, so when I say Miles was always there for us, I also mean he was always at home on the ranch.

Miles liked to study and took courses by mail. His first course was violin lessons. Miles had a violin. Here's how he got it:

The whole family was away from the ranch except Miles. A man (a stranger) drove in. Miles was no doubt glad for the company.

Miles was entertaining the gentleman and got out Dad's pearl-handled six-shooter to show him. Dad was very proud of that six-shooter. The whole family was proud of that pretty, pearl-handled six-shooter. It dated back to Dad's old fun days, the days he herded cattle for the Old Hundred and One outfit.

Before the stranger left, he had talked Miles into trading the forty-five with the pearl handle to him for a violin in its very own shabby violin case.

Needless to say, Dad was very unhappy over the deal, but what was done was done. Life had to go on.

Miles took lessons by mail on that violin for many months, or so it seemed to us who had to listen. He did not become a great violinist, but that violin is still in the family. His great grandson, Arlis Blake, has it now and plays it very well.

Miles' next project was lessons by mail on the cornet. Miles had picked up a cheap cornet some place. He did not become a musician on the cornet either, but I think it was good for his lungs. Each evening after the day's work and the chores were done and supper was over, Miles went up to his room and practiced his music. He was a lonesome teenager making the best of things.

After many, many months of working on his music, Miles ordered a course in electronics by mail.

Electronics he liked much better than music. He put his music stand away and moved his workshop down to the living room, using the library table for his workbench. Now, Bertie and I could watch Miles solder wires together and do all the other mysterious things he did. We were a part of his life again.

Of course, we had no electricity and Miles had to heat his soldering iron with a blowtorch. That was fun to watch.

When Miles began to build his Crystal Radio Set, we really got interested. The mail course had sent him all the parts. All Miles had to do was put them together in the right order.

Bertie and I watched with anticipation. We couldn't believe we would actually some day have a radio.

With the parts was a set of headphones. When the radio was all put together, Miles divided the headphones so two people could listen, each with one ear. He passed one earpiece around to each member of the family in turn. He kept one earpiece for himself so he could tune the radio. We heard a lot of static. We were thrilled.

Finally, one evening Miles heard a voice through the static. It was station KMMJ, Henry Fields in Iowa. I don't remember what year this was. I do know it was winter and our winter evenings were very interesting when we could listen to KKMJ two at a time.

Miles was always looking for something he could do on the side to make himself a little money. He saw an ad in a newspaper that told him to order several pairs of guinea pigs. It said they were easy to raise and multiplied rapidly. The Guinea Pig Company would buy all the guinea pigs he could raise. There was no way he could lose and think of all the fun it would be to watch those guinea pigs have little ones.

Miles ordered the however-many-they-told-him-he-needed. It wasn't long before a crate came up by mail with all those cute little fellows in it. They were all colors–black, white, brown, and spotted. We loved those little guinea pigs at first and we loved helping Miles with his livestock. The box they came in was their home. They could run around out in the yard, but they went home to sleep.

Multiply, they did. When they outgrew their box, we found them a bigger one until the guinea pig herd got so big they had to have their own building.

Miles and Mama decided to build a guinea pig house out of sod. (Dad was having nothing to do with them. If an animal couldn't be saddled, harnessed or butchered, he didn't see much use of having it on the place.)

Miles got the plow and harnessed a workhorse. Mama told Miles how deep to plow and how long to make the sod chunks. She showed him how to lay the sod to make a nice thick wall. She may have laid a few sods herself. As a kid she had no doubt watched the building of a few sod houses. She remembered how it used to be done.

Soon Miles had a nice, low, sod-tight building with a small opening for the little fellows to get inside for shelter. By this time, the grass in the south yard was so full of guinea pigs we had to watch where we stepped.

Billie and Bertie sitting on top of the sod guinea pig house.

Bertie and Me and Miles Too

All of our neighbors and friends had seen our cute little animals and Bertie and I had worn out our favorite joke we told to anyone seeing a guinea pig for the first time. We warned the visitor not to try to pick up a little one by his tail or his eyes would fall out. After seeing a few of the big fellows, they would realize guinea pigs have no tails. Then they'd know we'd pulled one on them.

Miles and Mama decided it was time to send some of those pigs back to the company they came from. Miles crated up a box of them and addressed it to company he had bought them from months ago. He sent them to town with the mailman.

Soon he got a freight bill from the Guinea Pig Company for the cost of shipping them back. They weren't buying guinea pigs.

Mama was very unhappy about that bill. She told Miles we wouldn't pay it.

We never heard from the guinea pig people again. I don't remember what happened to all those guinea pigs. I do know we used to sit on the little sod house out in the yard a lot.

Miles would rather fix something than break a saddle horse. In other words, he would rather fool with machinery than with horses. He could repair anything.

I remember summertime. Miles would be out in the yard tinkering with our old 1910 Ford. Bertie and I would be with him if Mama didn't have something for us to do. We watched him or did something nearby.

Miles was forever dropping a screw or a bolt or a nut into the grass. To us, helping Miles find this stuff was an important job. We tried to see which one of us could get it first. We got pretty good at finding tiny, little things in hard places.

Shortly after Miles was married, I was up at the ranch visiting. I saw his bride, Hollis, sitting on a sawhorse holding a wire under her arm while she embroidered a pillowcase. Miles was tinkering and needed a little help.

One time I was at the ranch seeing Mama and Dad. when Miles came in from the hayfield. He had stopped by the folks' place on the way to his house to see if they needed anything. Mama told him her gas refrigerator wasn't working. There was Miles down on the floor, fixing Mama's refrigerator while Hollis waited supper on him at their house.

When Dad ran the ranch, it was done entirely with horses and horse-drawn machines–a mowing machine with a six-foot sickle pulled by two horses, a fourteen-foot hayrake pulled by two horses, a sweep pulled by two horses, two horses for a stacker team. We used horses to haul the hay out to feed the cattle in the winter months. We needed saddle horses to work the cattle. Dad and the kids each had a saddle horse to ride the fences, that is, check all the pasture fences and make sure they were critter-tight. And, of course, there was the big, old lumber wagon and a team of horses for the loads and the big jobs, like picking up cow chips.

By the time Miles was doing most of the work, it was machinery. We might say, as Dad faded out, the horses went with him. Times changed. Dad couldn't have operated that way. His idea of fixing a motor was to kick it.

Miles loved machinery. He liked to tinker with it when it didn't work. He even got a small prop plane. Dad didn't want him to get it, but Miles went ahead. He learned to fly, bought the plane and built a small hanger at the end of an already level strip there by his house.

One of the family jokes was that Dad would not admit the plane was on the ranch. He wouldn't look at it or mention it.

One day Miles' small son Jimmy got the measles. (Jimmy was the apple of Dad's eye.) I went up to the ranch to help take care of Jimmy. I thought I was good at taking temperatures.

Jimmy's temperature was rising and I was taking it often. It was an old-fashioned thermometer with mercury in the tube and you had to "shake it down" before putting it under the tongue of the patient. It was good to have a certain flip to your wrist as you did this.

One morning I had too much determination in my wrist flip and dropped the thermometer and broke it. It was the only one we had.

Dad was there in the bedroom with me at the time. He turned and rushed out. I thought he was disgusted with me.

He soon was back in the house and said in fast words, "Bill, come and help Miles push the plane out of the hanger so he can fly to North Platte and get another thermometer."

Dad let Miles take him up in the plane just once, and that was to "save face" after Miles took Dad's brother George for a ride as a birthday gift when he turned ninety. Uncle George thought it was a great thrill. Dad didn't say a word. We all knew he'd rather keep his seat in the saddle and his feet on the ground.

Miles used the plane instead of a horse for many things. It made checking the windmills much easier and faster. Of course, if something needed done at once and it was too windy to take the plane up, Miles got on his trusty saddle horse and did the job. It never got too windy to do a job horseback.

Slowly the tractors took over all the jobs the work horses did. Dad enjoyed running the ranch his way. Miles enjoyed running it *his* way. Miles retired and his son Jim (Little Jimmy) took over. Jim enjoys running it *his* way, which is even more modern than Miles' method was.

This year, 2003, the ranch Dad started in 1903 will celebrate one hundred years. Jim and his wife Joyce will receive the award given by the Knights of Aksarben.

We kids (Miles, Nellie, Bertie and I) were happy to have been raised up there.

Miles, Little Jimmy and the Cessna.

Chapter Twenty-nine

Miles' Poem

Dad and Mama's first automobile was a 1910 two-seated, four passenger Ford with a wooden body. It had carbide headlights. A huge rubber ball beside the seat on the driver's side honked the brass horn that protruded from the front beside the engine. It had back doors but no front ones. That old car may have been the inspiration for Miles to write about Model T's.

Hollis, Miles' wife, told me he used to come in chuckling from the hayfields and say he had another verse for his poem and have her write it down. It took him all summer to finish it. It was published in the *Sutherland Courier*, August 10, 1961.

Ode to the Old Tin Lizzy
By Miles W. Snyder

I sometimes chuckle with mirthless glee
As I recall that contraption called a Model T.
It bounced and rattled and shook like hell,
While the kids all hollered and the wife did yell.

We used to think we were having fun
As we jigged along in the springtime sun,
Then all at once we'd have to stop,
And get all wet while we put up the top.

Some folks said, "They're the best in the land,
We can always push them out of the sand."
Others said, "They're fine for the mud
If you don't twist an axle or break a hub."

In winter weather we shivered for certain,
For there'd always be some holes in the curtain.
And we'd stop now and then to pump up a tire
Or make a small repair with some baling wire.

As we rattled along in the sonofa——
Trying hard to keep it out of the ditch,
And find some measure of motoring bliss
The darned old thing would begin to miss.

We'd stop at a garage to fix a coil
Buy five gallons of gas and a quart of oil,
Clean the plugs and put in some points,
Wipe off some grease and lube some joints.

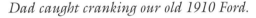

Dad caught cranking our old 1910 Ford.

1913 Model T (Photo courtesy of Jim Beckius)

Then for awhile it would hit on all four,
And smoke from the tailpipe would really pour,
Until a band would burn out and it wouldn't go.
Then we'd get a team and give it a tow.

When the "Mag" grew weak, the lights went dim.
If a tire went flat, we ran on the rim.
We jazzed the spark and tickled a coil,
And crawled underneath to check the oil.

We carried a pail to pour in water
To keep the engine from getting hotter,
Some extra oil we carried in a can
To replace that which dripped out of the pan.

If we wanted repair for the Model T Ford
We could get all we needed from "Monkey Ward."
If the ring gear happened to lose a cog,
We ordered another from the catalog.

We pushed on pedals for stops and starts,
The space in the rear was filled with parts;
For we carried extras by the score
Sometimes bought at the ten-cent store.

Unloading and assembling Ford Model T's.
(Photo courtesy of Jim Beckius)

And speaking of power, to get the most
We removed some lint from the magneto post.
Sometimes, to make the engine run a bit finer,
We stopped, got out and cleaned the timer.

Our face would get red, as with the coil box we fussed,
And we finally grew angry and audibly cussed.
For first 'twould be that, and then 'twould be this,
That made the old engine buck and miss.

Model T's used to be thick on the road,
And sometimes they carried a whale of a load;
Seed corn and machinery piled high and wide,
And maybe the bird-dog on the side.

Often you'd see, in his little old Ford,
A farmer with a can of cream on the running board,
Some boxes and bags, tied on the hood,
And in the back seat, a cord of wood.

The handiest thing we ever had on the farm,
Although now and then it might break our arm.
For this old car had a mind, so they said,
And if we lost our way home we just gave it its head.

Sometimes the wife would take it and go,
To a neighbors for club, or to town for a show.
At every fence she'd stop the old crate,
Get out and tug manfully at the gate.

Which was hard to open and harder to shut,
For prob'ly the brace wires had loosened up.
Then she'd get back in and on she'd go,
The first hundred feet pushing hard on low.

Clark Thornburg, Billie's husband Bob's Dad.

Then she'd let the old car back in "high,"
And on up the road she'd practically fly;
Until she'd get stalled in a steep sand bank
And have to get out and give the engine a crank.

Although the old Ford often gave us some trouble,
It would take us there, and back on the double.
And if the lights burned out on the old machine,
We hung out a lantern that burned kerosene.

And if we went out at night and got on a bender
And ran into a fence and crumpled a fender;
We'd just laugh and say, "There's no harm done,
'Cause now it matches the other one."

The Model T Ford could climb like a jeep,
If only the hills didn't get too steep;
For then the engine was sure to kill,
On account of gas, like water, doesn't run uphill.

Now the Model T Ford earned quite a name,
And shook plenty of hell out of many a dame.
'Twas often said, "I don't know what we'd have done
If we hadn't owned that old son of a gun."

Although the engine knocked and the drive shaft broke,
And it bore the brunt of many a joke;
The Model T Ford must've had what it takes;
For it far outsold all other makes.

1911 Tin Lizzie .
(Photo courtesy of Jim Beckius)

There were some who said, "It sure fills our needs."
Others complained, "It only has two speeds."
Some folks said they were fast and slow,
While others argued they were high and low.

But in nineteen hundred and twenty-eight
People demanded a car with a little more weight.
So Henry said, "To make this thing pay,
We will quit the T and begin the A."

So the little old car with the great big load
Slowly vanished from the road.
And there came a day when we'd seldom see
That contraption known as the Model T.

And they finally grew old and their number grew few
As they had to make way for something new.
But still once in awhile a T appears,
As bright and shiny as in former years.

Because there are some who like the old Ford,
And this little old car is being restored.
But 'twill no longer haul the monstrous loads
Nor clutter up the byways and roads.

So, no matter how we feel, the plain fact is,
We are not yet rid of the old "Tin Liz."
And it now looks as if, for a few more years,
There'll still be cars that don't shift gears.

Now, the little old Ford as it shines like new,
No longer black, but grey and blue.
From head lamp to tail lamp, from hubcap to dome,
It is glistening color and shining chrome.

Although it's the same old Ford as of years ago,
It's no longer for service but strictly for show.
'Twill no long transport the chickens and hogs,
A half dozen kids and two or three dogs.

For the little old T has earned a rest,
And now reposes inside with the very best.
No longer stock for a sight unseen trade,
It may strut its stuff in some fancy parade.

Yes, the Model T had what it took,
Though it rattled and bounced, shivered and shook.
And I really could go on and on,
About the old car that is almost gone.

But I hope, my friends, you have not been bored,
With this short history of the T Model Ford.
And I've no wish to be mean, for I'm no critic, you see,
And this is simply an ode to the old Model T.

Bob Thornburg's Uncle Alvin was proud of his new Model T.

From THE OLD 101 PRESS:

"They say you can't take it with you, but you can. When you die all the stories in your head go, too."

Billie Thornburg, founder of the Old Hundred and One Press and author of *Bertie and Me* and *Bertie and Me and Miles Too* is dedicated to encouraging people to write the stories of their lives. At age ninety she started **The Old Hundred and One Press** to publish history as told by those who've lived it.

Billie enjoys having people stop by 2220 Leota Street in North Platte, NE for an autographed copy of her book and to chat about writing. Or write your memories and send them to her to be included in a book she is compiling about the Midwest.

Send your contribution to:

The Old Hundred and One Press
13680 Sandhill Road
North Platte, NE 69101

www.theold101press.com
Phone: 308-534-0144

Have a complete manuscript? Let us help you self-publish. We offer editing, interior design, cover artwork, contract printing and promotion.

Available Now From The Old Hundred and One Press:

Bertie and Me, Billie Lee Snyder Thornburg's first book. A humorous and historical account of two little girls growing up on a Nebraska Sandhill ranch in the early 1900s.

Available in September 2003:

If Morning Never Comes by Bill VandenBush. The powerful story of a soldier's near-death experience in Vietnam. "A priceless gift to anyone in search of their own spiritual path...enormously inspirational." Nora Fitzgerald

Ask Me If I'm A Worm by Ann Milton. The second in a science series that teaches children about nature by comparing a kid's body to that of a worm. The first of the Ask Me Series, Ask Me If I'm A Frog, won the John Burroughs Nature Book Award.

Billie Thornburg is a living history lesson. She enjoys meeting with school children.as well as older people. Contact her through The Old Hundred and One Press to invite her to visit your school, library or retirement community.

Bill VandenBush is an inspiring speaker. He has appeared on Arthur C. Clark's *Mysterious Universe, Sightings, Town Meetings* and several near-death experience PBS specials. He has frequently shared his story at the International Association for Near Death Studies and with numerous community organizations, colleges, high schools and church groups. Contact him through The Old Hundred and One Press to invite him speak at your meeting, event or workshop.

Ann Milton delights in reading her interactive children's books to elementary kids of all ages and has a good time bringing out their creative abilities by writing with them. She is enthusiastic about sharing what she has learned about writing and self-publishing with anyone who will listen. Contact her through The Old Hundred and One Press.

ORDER FORM
for
Bertie and Me By Billie Lee Snyder Thornburg
Bertie and Me and Miles Too By Billie Lee Snyder Thornburg
If Morning Never Comes By Bill VandenBush
Ask Me If I'm A Worm By Ann Milton

Fax orders: 308-534-0145 *(Send this form)*
Telephone orders: 308-534-0144
Email orders: annmilton@inebraska.com
Postal orders: The Old Hundred and One Press
                13680 N Sandhill Road
                North Platte, NE 69101

Please send me _____ copies of **BERTIE and Me** *@ $18.95*
Please send me _____ copies of **BERTIE and Me and Miles Too** *@ $16.95*
Please send me _____ copies of **IF MORNING NEVER COMES** *@ $14.95*
Please send me _____ copies of **ASK ME IF I'M A WORM** *@ $8.95*

Add $4.00 for shipping and handling

TOTAL ENCLOSED: _____

Name:_____

Address:_____

City, State, ZIP: _____

Visit our website: www.theold101press.com